HUSKER TRIVIA

OFFICIALLY LICENSED COLLEGIATE PRODUCTS

NEBRASKA FOOTBALL QUIZ BOOK

LOWELL GREUNKE

HUSKER TRIVIA
Copyright © 1994 by ExHusker Press a division of Cross Training
Publishing

Library of Congress Cataloging-in-Publication Data

Greunke, Lowell
Lowell Greunke

Husker Trivia / Lowell Greunke
Published by ExHusker Press a division of Cross Training
Publishing, Grand Island, Nebraska 68803
Distributed in the United States and Canada by Cross Training
Publishing

Cover Illustrator: Jeff Sharpton
Printed in the United States of America

ISBN 1-885591-46-2

For additional books and resources available
through ExHusker Press contact us at:

ExHusker Press
a Division of
Cross Training Publishing
P.O. Box 1541
Grand Island, NE 68802
(308) 384-5762
ExHusker Press is owned and operated by Gordon Thiessen,
an ex-Husker, who played defensive end from 1975-80.

Dedication

This book is lovingly dedicated to the three most important people in my life. My wife, LaDonna, has been my best friend for over half of my life and she has made that life worth living. Laura, my bright and lovely daughter, encourages me with her energy and sunny outlook. Paul, my precious son, has taught me patience and hope through his positive reaction to adversity. I have truly been blessed three times over.

TABLE OF CONTENTS

Introduction

The devoted fans of the University of Nebraska-Lincoln football team are truly extraordinary in the big-business world of college athletics. Perhaps nowhere else in the United States can one find a single college team that affects the lives of a greater proportion of a state's populace. From the Panhandle to downtown Omaha hundreds of thousands of Nebraskans are vitally concerned about the success or failure of the Huskers. The team's exploits or prospects are prime topics of conversation 365 days a year. Whenever Husker fans get together, the conversation usually produces some reminiscing. The Game of the Century will often be discussed, or the two point conversion attempt against Miami in 1984, or the Bummeroosky, or a hundred other glorious (or disheartening) snippets of Husker lore.

I have been an ardent Husker fan for almost thirty-five years and I have often participated in conversations that dredged up bits of Big Red trivia, although to a true fan nothing about Husker football is really trivial. In this book I have attempted to jog the memories of Husker fans. Some of the questions posed in the various chapters are fairly easy to answer. Others will require quite a bit of thought. It is my fond hope that by testing yourself with these questions you can relive some exciting memories of seasons past. The questions cover the entire history of Nebraska football, from 1890 to the 1995 Orange Bowl game. Good luck with the questions. I hope that you will savor the memories that they will stimulate.

University of Nebraska
Football Office
Turner Gill

I recommend *Husker Trivia* to all true Cornhusker fans. It's a lot of fun to read and it's hard to put down once you get started guessing the answers.

I learned so much about the history of Nebraska football. Because I grew up in Texas, I had always heard so much more about Oklahoma and Texas teams. Therefore, it was interesting to learn more about the football program, here at Nebraska, that I chose for both my playing and coaching careers. It was also fun to remember all the players and games during my years here.

This book will provide many hours of enjoyable reading. It would also be entertaining to invite a group of Husker fans over and try to compare Husker knowledge.

1

HUSKER TRIVIA

NEBRASKA COACHES AND ASSISTANTS

1. In 1947 three of the six teams in the Big Six Conference had head coaches who had played at Nebraska. Who were these coaches?

2. Does Tom Osborne have a winning record against ranked opponents?

3. How many Big Six Conference titles did D.X. Bible's Nebraska teams win during his tenure?

4. Which Husker coach had the best career winning percentage while at Nebraska?

5. After the 1947 season, the University broke a coach's contract for the first time and a group of N.U. supporters bought up the remainder of the time left on the contract. Who was the victim of these maneuvers?

6. What is Bob Devaney's present position with the University of Nebraska?

7. Which Husker assistant coach left the team after the 1994 national championship season?

8. In the five year period from 1942 through 1946, how many different head coaches did Nebraska have?

9. Potsy Clark, N.U. head coach, introduced a new play called the South Platte Spread. What was this play?

1. Sam Francis coached Kansas in 1947. George Sauer led Kansas and, of course, Bernie Masterson coached at Nebraska.

2. Contrary to the perception of the national media, Osborne can win big games against ranked opponents. In his 22 seasons he has a 51-36-1 record, a 59% winning mark, against ranked foes.

3. Bible's teams won six conference titles—in 1929, 1931, 1932, 1933, 1935 and 1936.

4. E. O. "Jumbo" Stiehm, 1911-1915, had a .913 winning percentage with a 35-2-3 record at Nebraska.

5. Bernie Masterson was ousted under bitter circumstances after two seasons and only 5 victories against 13 defeats. He had a five year contract with the University but the remaining three years were bought up by a group of N.U. supporters.

6. He is officially Athletic Director Emeritus and since 1993 his primary function is fund-raising for the University.

7. Kevin Steele, Inside Linebackers Coach for the Husker for six seasons, received an offer he couldn't refuse. The expansion Carolina Panthers of the National Football League offered Steele the same coaching position that he had with the Huskers.

8. Nebraska went through four different head coaches during the period—1942—Glenn Presnell, 1943-44—A.J. Lewandowski, 1945—Potsy Clark, 1946—Bernie Masterson.

9. The blockers lined up at very wide intervals, almost from sideline to sideline. The ball was then snapped directly to the deep back who ran with the ball, if he could (which unfortunately wasn't very often).

10. Who is Nebraska's quarterbacks coach?

11. Bill Glassford had a pre-season camp where players endured strenuous training. Where was this camp?

12. D.X. Bible's teams had consistent trouble with only two teams. Who were these powerhouses that the Huskers could not defeat?

13. How many coaches did Tom Novak, Nebraska's great All-American, play under?

14. The same team handed both Bob Devaney and Tom Osborne their first losses as Nebraska head coach. Name the team.

15. Who is the only man to serve as head coach at Nebraska on two separate occasions?

16. Who coached Nebraska's football team to its most consecutive victories?

17. Which Nebraska coach holds the Big Eight record for most victories in the conference?

18. When Bernie Masterson took over as Nebraska head coach, he installed an offense that was patterned after a particular NFL team. What was the team and what was the offense that Masterson borrowed?

19. Which N.U. head coach was called "The Little Colonel?"

10. Turner Gill would seem to be the perfect coach to bring out the best in Husker signal callers. After all, Nebraska has spent the last decade searching for the second coming of Turner Gill and every quarterback since 1983 has been measured against his accomplishments.

11. The Huskers got ready for the season at Curtis, Nebraska in the southwestern section of the state. There the players were put through training that would have made the Marines proud.

12. D.X. Bible was 0-4-0 against Minnesota and 0-6-2 against Pittsburgh. The 10 losses were 2/3 of his teams' total losses during his coaching tenure.

13. Novak had three different mentors—1946-7, Bernie Masterson, 1948, Potsy Clark and 1949, Bill Glassford.

14. The Missouri Tigers were a perennial thorn for Huskers during the 1960s and 1970s. They defeated Devaney's 1962 team 16-7 and Osborne's 1973 team 13-12.

15. George "Potsy" Clark was coach in 1945 with a 4-5-0 record and again in 1948 with a 2-8-0 record.

16. Walter C. "Bummy" Booth led the Huskers to 27 straight victories from 1901 to 1904.

17. Tom Osborne continues to extend his record victory total with 219 wins as of the end of the 1994 season.

18. Masterson installed the T-formation that he had utilized as quarterback for seven years of the Chicago Bears. The formation proved to be essentially unsuccessful for the Huskers.

19. D.X. Bible, head coach at Nebraska, 1929-36, was known by this colorful nickname.

20. Nebraska has had three head coaches who had earlier played for the Huskers. Who were these men?

21. How does Tom Osborne's winning percentage compare to other Division 1-A coaches?

22. Why did Biff Jones leave the head coaching job at Nebraska in 1941?

23. What was Bill Jennings' greatest victory during his ill-fated stint as head coach at Nebraska?

24. Which Nebraska coach won the most conference titles?

25. When Bob Devaney stepped down as Nebraska's Athletic Director in 1993, who replaced him?

26. Which Husker coach has served the longest in that capacity at the University?

27. Which Husker coach holds the school record for most victories?

28. What was the most surprising loss by a Devaney-coached N.U. team?

20. Glenn Presnell coached in 1942 and lettered 1925-27. A.J. Lewandowski coached in 1943-44 and lettered 1928-29. Bernie Masterson coached in 1946 and lettered 1931-33.

21. Osborne in 1993 reclaimed the title of winningest active coach from John Robinson of Southern California. His teams have won a remarkable 82% of their games over the past 22 years (219 wins, 47 losses, three ties).

22. Jones was an army major and he was recalled into active service after the end of the 1941 season.

23. Without question his stunning upset of powerful Oklahoma stands out as the high water mark of his career at N.U. The Huskers managed back-to-back victories over the Sooners, 25-21 in 1959 and 17-14 in 1960. Unfortunately, Jennings experienced only 13 other victories in his five seasons at Nebraska.

24. Tom Osborne's teams have claimed the most conference titles during his tenure as head coach. His Husker teams have won seven outright Big Eight titles and also have earned four co-championships during his 22 years as head coach at Nebraska.

25. On January 4, 1993 Devaney turned over the administrative reigns to Bill Byrne.

26. Dr. Tom Osborne extends his record as he begins his 23rd year as head coach of the Cornhuskers in September 1995.

27. Tom Osborne holds the record with 219 victories in 22 years at the helm. His overall record is 219-47-3.

28. Perhaps the most unexpected loss was the 12-0 shutout in 1968 by Kansas State, a team which had not won a conference game in 14 starts.

29. Besides being head football coach, what other duty does Tom Osborne have within the University of Nebraska athletic department?

30. What was Nebraska's first non-conference loss under Bob Devaney?

31. How many consecutive losses did Bob Devaney experience as head coach at Nebraska?

32. Why did Devaney stay on as head coach through the 1972 season even though his successor had already been named?

33. Which Nebraska coach holds the Big Eight record for number of games coached?

34. When did Bob Devaney become Nebraska's athletic director in addition to his duties as head football coach?

35. How many times was Bob Devaney named Big Eight Coach of the Year?

36. How many times were Bob Devaney's Huskers shut out and by whom?

37. When Tom Osborne won his 200th game in 1993, he joined two other active coaches in reaching this lofty plateau. Name these coaches.

38. Was Bob Devaney ever named National Coach of the Year?

29. Osborne is also an assistant athletic director for the University of Nebraska.

30. The first non-conference loss under Bob Devaney was the 17-13 setback in 1963 to the Air Force Academy. By the way, this was the only blemish on N.U.'s 10-1-0 season record for 1963.

31. Devaney endured 2 consecutive losses four times at Nebraska—once in 1966, twice in 1967 and once in 1968.

32. Devaney sought an accomplishment no other coach had attained. He wanted to win three consecutive national championships. Unfortunately, it was not to be for Nebraska or Devaney.

33. Tom Osborne continues to add to his record each years as his conference total reached 269 games coached as of the 1995 Orange Bowl.

34. Devaney became athletic director in 1967 after the resignation of Tippy Dye.

35. He was honored as Big Eight Coach of the Year five times— in 1962, 1963, 1964, 1970 and 1971.

36. They were blanked 3 times—once in 1967, 10-0 by Kansas and twice in 1968, 12-0 by Kansas State and 47-0 by Oklahoma.

37. Two of Osborne's coaching friends, Bobby Bowden of Florida State and Joe Paterno of Penn State, reached the elite 200 win level prior to Tom Osborne.

38. No, despite two national championships and a fantastic winning record, the Coach of the Year honor is about the only accolade that eluded Bob Devaney during his coaching career.

39. For which college did Bob Devaney play football?

40. How many times have Tom Osborne's Huskers lost to unranked opponents in his 21 years as head coach at Nebraska?

41. What was N.U.'s largest margin of defeat under Bob Devaney?

42. Who gave the recommendation to Clifford Hardin, N.U.'s chancellor, to approach Bob Devaney about the head coaching job at Nebraska?

43. How long had Devaney coached at Wyoming before he came to Nebraska in 1962?

44. Who is the only Nebraska coach to defeat a No. 1 team?

45. What was Bob Devaney's prior position before he got his first college head coaching job at Wyoming?

46. Who was the athletic director at N.U. when Bob Devaney was hired as head coach?

47. Which was the first team to defeat the Huskers after Bob Devaney took over as head coach?

48. Who was Tom Osborne's roommate when he played professional football with the San Francisco 49'ers?

39. Bob Devaney had been an all-conference end and MVP for Alma College in Michigan. He was the captain of his team and graduated in 1939.

40. The loss to Iowa State in 1992 marked just the 11th loss to an unranked opponent in Osborne's tenure at Nebraska.

41. Nebraska was literally crushed 47-0 by Oklahoma in 1968, the second of two consecutive 6-4-0 seasons for Devaney's Huskers.

42. Duffy Daugherty, head coach at Michigan State recommended Devaney for the job. Duffy and Bob had worked together at Michigan State.

43. Devaney had spent 5 years as the head coach of the Cowboys. While at Wyoming, he had compiled a record of 35 wins, 10 losses and 5 ties.

44. Tom Osborne's 1978 team managed to beat No. 1 Oklahoma, 17-14, in a game that was also his first victory over the Sooners as Nebraska's head coach.

45. Devaney was an assistant coach at Michigan State under his friend, Duffy Daugherty.

46. The athletic director was Tippy Dye, himself newly hired for the job.

47. The Missouri Tigers beat the Huskers 16-7 on November 3, 1962.

48. His roommate was none other than Jack Kemp the former Congressman, presidential candidate and Secretary of Housing and Urban Development in the Bush administration.

49. Did a Bob Devaney-coached Nebraska team ever lose to an opponent who finished the season with a losing record?

50. Devaney's N.U. teams had two ties during his tenure as head coach. What were these two ties?

51. Tom Osborne's N.U. teams have been tied three times. By whom were they tied?

52. Who is the only remaining member of Tom Osborne's first Husker staff?

53. What position did Tom Osborne play at Hastings College?

54. During Tom Osborne's years as head coach, how many teams has N.U. met in bowl games that they had never ever played before?

55. At which school was Turner Gill an assistant coach before returning to Nebraska?

56. How many times in a row did Osborne's Nebraska teams lose to Oklahoma before they finally notched a victory?

57. Half of the Big Eight coaches left at the end of the 1994 season. Name them.

58. Jerry Moore, an N.U. assistant coach, left the Huskers to become head coach at which school?

49. Yes, Devaney coached one Husker team to a defeat against a team which finished with a losing record for the season. Nebraska lost to Kansas State 12-0 in 1968 and the Wildcats ended the season with a 4-6-0 record.

50. The Huskers were tied 21-21 by Southern California in 1970 and 23-23 by Iowa State in 1972.

51. The Huskers have been tied by Oklahoma State 17-17 in 1973, by L.S.U. 6-6 in 1976 and by Colorado 19-19 in 1991.

52. George Darlington is the old timer among the Husker assistant coaches, having logged 22 seasons as of the 1994 campaign.

53. Osborne was a star quarterback for Hastings. The Omaha World-Herald named Osborne its College Athlete of the Year in 1959.

54. They have met 8 teams for the first time—Florida, Arizona State, Texas Tech, North Carolina, Houston, Mississippi State, Clemson and Georgia Tech.

55. Turner was a graduate assistant and then full-time assistant coach at Southern Methodist University before coming to Nebraska as quarterbacks coach in 1992.

56. Tom's Huskers lost five straight to the Sooners, 1973-77, before Nebraska finally won 17-14 in 1978.

57. Three expected departures were Gary Gibbs of Oklahoma, Jim Walden of Iowa State and Pat Jones at Oklahoma State. More shocking was the resignation of Colorado's Bill McCartney after a very successful career with the Buffaloes.

58. Moore became head coach at North Texas State in 1979.

59. How long was Bob Devaney the athletic director at Nebraska?

60. After which season did Tom Osborne seriously think about leaving Nebraska and which school was trying to woo him away?

61. What is the fewest number of games Nebraska has won in the regular season under Tom Osborne and how many times has this happened?

62. Which Husker coach produced the first Nebraska All-American players?

63. Five times in Osborne's career his Husker teams have suffered two consecutive defeats to end the season. When did this happen?

64. How many times have Tom Osborne's teams won the Big Eight championship?

65. When was Tom Osborne's first undisputed Big Eight championship?

66. Which 1965 Husker co-captain later became a Nebraska assistant coach?

59. Devaney took over the athletic director position from Tippy Dye in 1967 and served until 1992. During his 25 year tenure all Nebraska athletic programs were strengthened.

60. After the 1978 season, Colorado offered Osborne the head coaching position. He turned it down and subsequently Chuck Fairbanks took the Colorado job. Osborne went on to greater success with the Huskers.

61. The Huskers have won 8 games under Coach Osborne 4 times in the regular season—in 1973, 1974, 1976 and 1977.

62. "Jumbo" Stiehm coached two All-Americans, Vic Halligan in 1914 and Guy Chamberlin in 1915.

63. In 1975 Nebraska lost to Oklahoma 35-10 and then to Arizona State 17-14 in the Fiesta Bowl. In 1978 N.U. lost to Missouri 35-31 and then to Oklahoma 31-24 in the Orange Bowl. In 1979 Nebraska lost to Oklahoma 17-14 and then to Houston 17-14 in the Cotton Bowl. In 1985 Nebraska lost to Oklahoma 27-7 and then to Michigan 27-23 in the Fiesta Bowl. In 1990 N.U. lost to Oklahoma 45-10 and then to Georgia Tech 45-21 in the Florida Citrus Bowl.

64. Nebraska has won seven titles outright, 1981-83, 1988 and 1992-4 and four conference co-championships, 1975, 1978, 1984 and 1991 in Osborne's 22 years as Husker head coach.

65. Osborne's 1981 team was the first to win the championship outright. He then won three consecutive championships, 1981-83.

66. Frank Solich, a great Husker fullback and co-captain, now is assistant head coach and heir-apparent to Tom Osborne.

67. During his tenure as assistant head coach, Tom Osborne actually was also an instructor at the University. What subject did he teach?

68. What is the biggest margin of defeat a Tom Osborne team has endured and who was the perpetrator?

69. How old was Tom Osborne when he took over as head coach of the Nebraska Cornhuskers?

70. Name the three sportswriters from Lincoln who assisted Bob Devaney in writing his autobiography.

71. Tom Osborne lost his first game at Nebraska in a manner which should sound familiar to fans after the outcome of the 1984 Orange Bowl. What happened?

72. When did Tom Osborne join the coaching staff at Nebraska?

73. In one season under Tom Osborne, the Huskers lost two consecutive games by the same score. What was the score and what was the season?

74. One of the Florida schools tried to hire Bob Devaney as football coach after the 1963 season. Which school tried to steal him away from Nebraska?

75. Nebraska went three years without a season opening victory under coach Osborne. In what seasons did N.U. suffer these failures and against which teams?

67. Osborne was an instructor in educational psychology, a field in which he has a doctorate.

68. As you might have guessed, the Oklahoma Sooners did it to the Huskers. In 1990 they whipped Nebraska 45-10 for a winning margin of 35 points.

69. When he was named as Devaney's successor at Nebraska, Tom Osborne was only 34 years old, which is quite young for a head coach at a major university.

70. They were Randy York, Mike Babcock and Virgil Parker of the Lincoln Journal and Lincoln Star.

71. In the fifth game of the 1973 season, Missouri had gone ahead of Nebraska late in the game, 13-6. The Huskers scored but lost the game on a failed two point conversion, similar to the fate they suffered against Miami of Florida.

72. He started as an unpaid assistant in 1962. Osborne returned to Nebraska after a three year professional career with the Washington Redskins and the San Francisco 49ers.

73. In 1979 N.U. lost to Oklahoma by a 17-14 score and then lost to Houston in the Cotton Bowl by the identical score.

74. Miami was interested in having Devaney do for the Hurricanes what he had done for the Huskers. Fortunately, the job wasn't nearly as attractive as it is now and Devaney decided to stay at Nebraska.

75. The Huskers tied L.S.U. at Baton Rouge 6-6 in 1976, lost to Washington State in Lincoln 19-10 in 1977 and lost to Alabama in Birmingham 20-3 in 1978.

76. An Osborne-coached Husker team has been shut out only twice. Against whom did this happen and in which seasons did it take place?

77. In which subject does Tom Osborne have his Ph.D degree?

78. Which school almost hired away assistant coach Ron Brown after the 1993 season?

79. Has a Tom Osborne team ever lost to an opponent who has finished the season with a losing record?

80. When Warren Powers, an ex-Nebraska assistant coach, left Washington State to take over at Missouri, another ex-Nebraska assistant took over as Washington State coach. Who is he?

81. Who has made Nebraska's weight training program the model for all of college football?

82. Who was the tough, crusty assistant coach who developed so many fine running backs for Bob Devaney and Tom Osborne?

83. What has been the Husker's longest winning streak under Tom Osborne?

84. What is the name of Tom Osborne's autobiography?

76. Oklahoma, Dr. Tom's old nemesis, shut the Huskers down completely 27-0 in 1973, Osborne's first season as head coach at Nebraska. N.U. crossed midfield only once and then fumbled on the play. 221 games later Miami dominated the Huskers 22-0 in the 1992 Orange Bowl.

77. Osborne earned his doctorate in educational psychology and for several years taught courses in that subject in addition to his duties as an assistant football coach.

78. None other than Bobby Bowden and Florida State wanted Brown to work with the Seminole receivers. Brown decided that he had unfinished business at Nebraska and opted to remain with the Huskers.

79. Yes, Nebraska was defeated by Iowa State 19-10 in 1992 in a shocking upset. The Cyclones finished the season with a losing record. The upset was perhaps the biggest of the 1992 football season.

80. Jim Walden took over as head coach at Washington State in 1978 before moving on to Iowa State.

81. Boyd Epley has made the Nebraska weight program the envy of all other college teams and many pro teams.

82. Many of the backs learned the hard way with Mike Corgan but he brought out the best in them, both on the field and off.

83. The longest winning streak has been 22 games from the 1982 27-24 loss to Penn State to the 1984 loss to Miami in the Orange Bowl.

84. His 1985 book, entitled "More Than Winning," truly represents his philosophy of life.

85. Which Nebraska coach has lost the most bowl games in his career?

86. How many years did John Melton serve as a Husker assistant coach and what position did he coach?

87. Among the all-time Division 1-A leaders in wins, where does Nebraska's Tom Osborne rank?

85. Tom Osborne set this national record, 13, with Nebraska's loss to Florida State in the 1994 Orange Bowl. Osborne passed up Bo Schembechler and Bear Bryant with this loss.

86. John Melton retired after the 1988 season, having served as an assistant coach for 27 years. He ended his career as the linebackers coach and he taught some great ones during his tenure.

87. Osborne, with 219 victories through the end of the 1994 season, ranks 8th all-time. The next coach he will pass is Bo Schembechler with 234 victories.

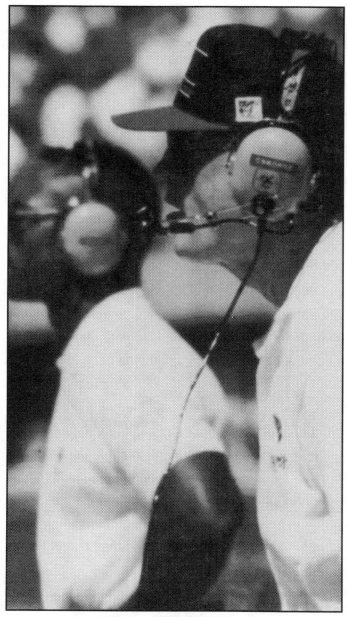

Tom Osborne

2

QUARTERBACKS

88. Who was the student manager who actually saw action as quarterback in a 1994 game because of the shortage of quarterbacks?

89. Which Husker quarterback attempted the most passes in one game for N.U.?

90. Which quarterback holds the school record for best passing percentage in one game at Nebraska?

91. Why didn't Vince Ferragamo have a part in the 1975 season opener against L.S.U.?

92. Which Husker quarterback had the most rushing carries in a season?

93. Which quarterback established the school mark for touchdown/interception ratio and during which season was the record set?

94. Which Husker quarterback holds the record for most passes completed in one game at N.U.?

95. Who started at quarterback for Tom Osborne's first game as head coach at Nebraska?

96. Name the Husker quarterback who threw the longest touchdown pass in N.U. football history.

88. Freshman Adam Kucera played quarterback on the scout team because other quarterbacks were hurt or had left the team. He actually took a few snaps in the lopsided 70-21 massacre of lowly Pacific.

89. Dave Humm established the mark of 42 pass attempts against Iowa State in 1972.

90. The great Turner Gill established the record with a phenomenal 11 for 12 performance against Kansas State in 1982 which translates into a .917 pass completion record.

91. He and three other players had been sentenced to a one game suspension because N.U. had taken them as scout team members to the 1974 Sugar Bowl game, an NCAA rule violation. Senior Terry Luck played fairly well in the L.S.U. game and Nebraska held on to win 10-7.

92. Steve Taylor carried the ball 157 times in 1988.

93. Amazingly Tommie Frazier had a splendid freshman campaign in 1992 in which he tossed 10 touchdown passes and had only one pass picked off, for a 10 to 1 ratio.

94. Dave Humm completed 25 passes in a game against Wisconsin in 1973. He went 25 for 36 for 297 yards and two touchdowns against the Badgers.

95. Steve Runty stepped in when first team quarterback Dave Humm hurt his knee. Runty made the most of his starting opportunity, completing 9 of 11 passes for 105 yards and one score. He led the Huskers to a 40-13 pasting of the U.C.L.A Bruins.

96. Fred Duda tossed a pass to his old reliable end, Freeman White, who streaked 95 yards for a score against Colorado in 1965.

97. Which N.U. quarterback had the most rushing attempts in his career?

98. Which Nebraska quarterback from Omaha never rose higher than third string during his 5 years as a Husker yet managed to play three years of professional football?

99. Which Husker quarterback threw the most interceptions in his career?

100. Who holds the school record for most pass completions in one season at N.U.?

101. Which N.U. quarterback set the Big Eight record for lowest pass interception percentage in a career?

102. Which Husker quarterback had the most consecutive pass attempts without an interception?

103. Who holds the N.U. school record for most yards passing in one season?

104. What injury sidelined Tommie Frazier for much of the 1994 season?

105. In 1992 Tommie Frazier only had one pass intercepted in the regular season. Against which team did he turn the ball over?

106. Name the Husker quarterback who gained the most yards rushing in one game.

97. Steve Taylor had 431 carries for 2125 yards in his N.U. career, 1985-88.

98. Ed Burns, always a crowd favorite, did letter at Nebraska in 1977 and played for the New Orleans Saints, 1978-80.

99. Dave Humm holds most of the Husker passing records and he set this one also. In his Nebraska career, 1972-74, Humm was intercepted 36 times.

100. Vince Ferragamo established the mark of 145 pass completions in 1976. He attempted 254 passes during the season.

101. Turner Gill set the record of 2.57% (11 interceptions in 428 attempts) during his N.U. career. He broke Jerry Tagge's mark.

102. Turner Gill had 125 pass attempts without an interception. The string lasted 12 games from the Colorado game of 1982 to the Syracuse game of 1983.

103. Dave Humm set the school record in 1972 when he passed for 2074 yards.

104. A blood clot developed behind Frazier's right knee. This injury kept Frazier out of action for most of the 1994 season. He returned to action in the 1995 Orange Bowl victory.

105. It was perhaps fitting that the Huskers' old-time nemesis Oklahoma would be the team to pick off Tommie's pass.

106. Gerry Gdowski gained 174 yards against Iowa State in 1989 to set the record.

107. Which quarterback holds the record for best passing percentage for a career at Nebraska?

108. Nebraska lost only two games during the 1981-83 seasons in which Turner Gill was the starting quarterback. Name those two games.

109. Which Nebraska quarterback holds the school record for passing yardage in one game?

110. Which N.U. quarterback gained the most rushing yards in one season?

111. Who tied a Husker record with three touchdown tosses and added another rushing score in the 1985 28-10 Sugar Bowl victory over L.S.U.?

112. What famous Nebraska quarterback hailed from Green Bay, Wisconsin?

113. Why was Tommie Frazier denied a medical hardship exemption after his blood clot problem in 1994?

114. Which Husker quarterback set the school record for rushing yards gained in a career?

115. What position did quarterback Turner Gill play on Nebraska's baseball team?

116. Which Husker quarterback scored the most rushing touchdowns in his career?

107. Jerry Tagge completed 348 of his 581 pass attempts during his career at N.U. which spanned 1969-71. This translates into a very fine .598 pass completion rate.

108. The Huskers lost only a 27-24 decision to Penn State in 1982 and a 31-30 decision in the 1984 Orange Bowl to Miami of Florida. Both losses kept the Nebraska team from claiming the national championship in those seasons.

109. Dave Humm established the one game mark of 297 yards against Wisconsin in 1973.

110. Gerry Gdowski gained 925 yards in 1989.

111. Quarterback Craig Sundberg played one of his finest games and was named MVP for his performance.

112. Jerry Tagge, who lettered 1969-71 and led N.U. to two consecutive national titles, was a lifelong Green Bay Packer fan and went on to play at quarterback for the team after his Husker play was finished.

113. The NCAA denied his appeal because Frazier played in two series of the Pacific game. Frazier appeared in just slightly over the allowed percentage of his team's games. The NCAA would not make an exception in Frazier's case and grant him another year of eligibility.

114. The great Steve Taylor established the quarterback mark with 2125 yards gained in his Husker career, 1985-88.

115. Gill, drafted by the Chicago White Sox after high school, played shortstop for the Husker baseball team.

116. Steve Taylor scored 32 rushing touchdowns in his N.U. career, 1985-88 to establish the school record.

117. Who was the first true freshman to start at quarterback at Nebraska?

118. Which Husker quarterback set the record for the most passes attempted in a season at N.U.?

119. What injury sidelined quarterback Brook Berringer for portions of two games in 1994?

120. Who holds the school record for most pass completions in a career at N.U.?

121. Who was Nebraska's first regular black quarterback?

122. Which Husker quarterback scored the most rushing touchdowns in one game?

123. After Turner Gill ended his Husker career, where did he play professional football?

124. Which quarterback at N.U. has thrown the most touchdown passes in one game?

125. Vince Ferragamo transferred to Nebraska from the University of California after competing with another All-American quarterback. Both became professional quarterbacks. Who is this old competitor?

117. Though other freshmen have in the past played in some games, Tommie Frazier was the first true freshman quarterback to be given the starting nod at Nebraska. This is a testament to his remarkable athletic skills.

118. Dave Humm established the standard in 1972 when he attempted 266 passes.

119. Brook played the second half of the Wyoming game with a collapsed lung. He reinjured the lung in the Oklahoma State game and didn't return until the second half of the Kansas State game.

120. Dave Humm established the completion mark with 353 during his career which went from 1972 to 1974.

121. Turner Gill started for most of three seasons, 1981-83. Other black quarterbacks had played at N.U., but Gill was the first to start several games.

122. Gerry Gdowski scored four touchdowns against Iowa State in 1989 and Mickey Joseph matched the record against Missouri in 1990.

123. Gill had a successful stint with the Montreal Concordes of the Canadian Football League (1984-85), before recurring concussions forced him to give up football for health reasons.

124. Steve Taylor was incredible in the Sept. 12, 1987 game versus U.C.L.A.. He tossed 5 touchdown passes in that game.

125. Steve Bartkowski, later of the Atlanta Falcons was Ferragamo's old nemesis at California. Both went on to fame and fortune in the National Football League.

126. Which Husker quarterback threw for the most touchdowns in a season at Nebraska?

127. Frank Patrick had been N.U.'s quarterback in 1967 and 1968. Where was he shifted in 1969?

128. Name the Husker quarterback who scored the most rushing touchdowns in a season.

129. After Turner Gill quit professional football, did he give up professional athletics?

130. In which game did Turner Gill injure his leg, an injury which almost ended his N.U. career?

131. Which Nebraska quarterback attempted the most passes in his career at Nebraska?

132. Who took over for the injured Turner Gill in the 1981 Oklahoma game and guided the Huskers to a decisive 37-14 victory?

133. In the 1967 freshman season, who started as the first team quarterback of the Huskers?

134. Which quarterback holds the N.U. school record for most passing yardage during his career?

126. Vince Ferragamo set the passing mark with 20 TDs in 1976.

127. With the arrival of Jerry Tagge and Van Brownson on the scene, Patrick's role as quarterback was diminished. It was decided that he should be shifted to tight end in 1969.

128. Steve Taylor scored 13 rushing TDs in 1988 and Gerry Gdowski matched that record in 1989.

129. No, Gill then gave professional baseball a try and spent three years (1986-88) in the Cleveland and Detroit minor league baseball systems.

130. Gill injured his leg in the 1981 Iowa State game. He took a blow to his right leg in the first quarter but continued to play until the fourth quarter. Two operations followed and a long, anxious wait to see if his leg nerves would regenerate.

131. Dave Humm set the record for pass attempts in his career when he launched 637 from 1972-74.

132. Mark Mauer led the Husker troops expertly in the thrashing of the Sooners. He was 11 for 16 in passing for 148 yards and one touchdown. He also provided the field leadership to his teammates on numerous long touchdown drives.

133. Surprisingly, Jeff Kinney began the season as the first team quarterback of the yearlings. He later found the spotlight as one of Nebraska's greatest running backs.

134. Dave Humm, who holds most of the passing records at Nebraska, also owns this record as he passed for 5035 yards during his N.U. career, 1972-74.

135. Who took over and performed superbly in the first game of the 1993 season when Tommie Frazier was injured after two snaps?

136. What is significant about the fact that Jerry Tagge was drafted by the Green Bay Packers in 1972?

137. Which Husker quarterback threw for the most touchdowns in his career?

138. In the ranking of season pass attempts, one quarterback holds 3 of the top 6 listings. Who is this quarterback?

139. Which N.U. quarterback had the most rushing carries in a game?

140. Dave Humm's 353 pass completions in his career broke whose school record?

141. Vince Ferragamo's record 145 pass completions in 1976 broke whose season record at N.U.?

142. When Dave Humm established the school record for career pass attempts, whose record did he break?

143. In 1994 who was the first walk-on to start at quarterback for Nebraska since Travis Turner in 1985?

135. Brook Berringer had his finest game against North Texas when Tommie Frazier went down with an ankle sprain. Berringer went 7 for 7 in passing for 124 yards and one touchdown.

136. What is interesting is the fact that Tagge grew up in Green Bay and was a lifelong Packer fan.

137. Dave Humm established the record with 41 TD passes during his career at Nebraska, 1972-74.

138. Dave Humm ranks 1st with 266 attempts in 1972, 4th with 196 attempts in 1973 and 6th with 175 attempts in 1974.

139. John Bordogna rushed 25 times for 143 yards against Iowa State in 1952.

140. Jerry Tagge had held the previous record with 348 pass completions during his career, 1969-71.

141. Jerry Tagge had established the former mark with 143 completions in the championship season of 1971 and Dave Humm had matched the record in 1973.

142. Humm, who attempted 637 passes in his career at Nebraska, shattered the mark of Jerry Tagge who attempted 581 passes, 1969-71.

143. With Tommie Frazier and Brook Berringer injured, sophomore Matt Turman got the starting call against 11th ranked Kansas State in Manhattan. He played well and Nebraska prevailed 17-6 with a tremendous defensive effort.

Turner Gill

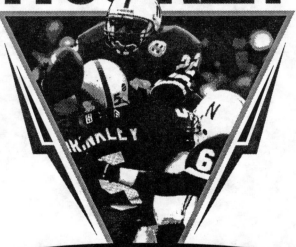

3

RUNNING BACKS

144. A former Nebraska back who played on Bob Devaney's first N.U. team in 1962 went on to be a head coach and produced some heartbreaking losses for Tom Osborne. Who is he?

145. Name the N.U. player who scored the most rushing touchdowns in one seasons by a fullback.

146. Which Nebraska player set the school record the most net yards gained rushing in his career?

147. Before walking on at Nebraska, fullback Mark Schellen played football at another school. Which one?

148. Which Husker player scored the most rushing touchdowns in his career?

149. How quickly did Lawrence Phillips reach 1,000 yards rushing in 1994?

150. Name the Husker player who had the longest touchdown run in N.U. football history.

151. How many times since 1978 has Nebraska failed to produce a 1000 yard rusher?

152. Mike Rozier shattered an old Big Eight record for most points scored in a season. How many points did he score and whose record did he break?

144. Warren Powers, one of Devaney's halfbacks, coached Washington State to an upset victory over Nebraska in 1977 and led the Missouri Tigers to a similar win in 1978.

145. Mark Schellen scored 9 rushing touchdowns in 1983.

146. Mike Rozier gained 4780 yards in his Husker career, 1981-83. The old record was 2814 yards gained by I.M. Hipp, 1977-79.

147. Schellen started for one year at the University of Nebraska at Omaha. He then quit school for a year before giving football one last try at Nebraska.

148. Mike Rozier scored 49 rushing touchdowns in his N.U. career, 1981-83, to establish the school record.

149. He achieved this plateau in six games. It took Mike Rozier seven games to reach 1,000 yards rushing in 1983.

150. Actually two players tied for the distinction. Craig Johnson set the record in 1979 with a 94 yard run against Kansas and Roger Craig matched that performance with a 94 yard gallop against Florida State in 1981.

151. In the past 16 years only twice have the Huskers failed to reach this plateau, in 1986 and 1990. This is a true testament to Nebraska's rushing might.

152. Rozier scored 174 points in 1983 to crush the previous record of 157 points established by Bobby Reynolds of Nebraska in 1950. However, it must be remembered that Reynolds scored his points in nine games and Rozier played in twelve games.

153. Which Husker player scored the most rushing touchdowns in one season?

154. Who was Tom Osborne's first I-back?

155. Who kept Lawrence Phillips from being the leading Big Eight rusher in 1994?

156. In 1978, counting the Orange Bowl game, the Huskers had two running backs who each gained more than 1000 yards rushing. Who were they?

157. Who established Nebraska's single game rushing record by a running back?

158. In 1976 a sophomore I-back was Nebraska's leading rusher. Who was he?

159. Who was the last Husker fullback to lead the team in rushing during a season?

160. One might think that Jeff Kinney was the leading rusher on the national championship team of 1970. He wasn't. Who was the team leader?

161. Name the Husker I-back or halfback who had the most rushing attempts in his career.

162. In what game was Jarvis Redwine's knee injured away from a play?

153. Mike Rozier scored an incredible 29 rushing touchdowns in 1983.

154. Tony Davis, from Tecumseh, made a great entrance against U.C.L.A. in 1973. He gained 147 yards rushing on 24 carries, caught 3 passes for 32 yards and scored 2 touchdowns.

155. Heisman Trophy winner Rashaan Salaam gained more than 2,000 yards in 1994 and, of course, was the Big Eight rushing leader.

156. Rick Berns had 1032 yards rushing and I.M. Hipp added 1002 yards.

157. Calvin Jones broke the great Mike Rozier's record by gaining 294 yards against Kansas in 1991. In addition, Calvin hadn't even started the game!!

158. Rick Berns gained 854 yards in 1976 to lead the Huskers in rushing.

159. It has been a long time, 22 years to be exact, since a fullback has led the Huskers in rushing. Tough Tony Davis gained 1,008 yards on 254 carries in 1973.

160. Joe Orduna had 834 yards during the regular season to lead the Huskers in rushing in 1970.

161. Mike Rozier had 668 rushing attempts in his productive Husker career, 1981-83.

162. Redwine took a direct shot in the knees by a Missouri defender on an N.U. extra point attempt in the second quarter of the 1979 game in which the Huskers squeaked to a 23-20 win. This injury contributed to some "bad blood" between the Huskers and the Tigers during the next few seasons.

163. Name the Husker running back who had the best average gain per rushing carry in a career.

164. Who was Nebraska's leading rusher in 1972, Bob Devaney's last year as head coach?

165. Which N.U. running back holds the school record for the highest average gain per carry in a season?

166. Which modern N.U. running back, excluding quarterbacks, lost the most yards rushing in his career?

167. Frank Solich has coached the Husker running backs for 11 seasons. In how many seasons has he tutored an All-Big Eight running back?

168. Name the Nebraska fullback who set the school record for rushing attempts in one game.

169. Lawrence Phillips established the school record for consecutive 100-plus-yard games to start a season. How many did he have?

170. When Mike Rozier broke the Big Eight record for rushing yards gained in a career, whose record did he break?

171. Which Husker running back had the most rushing attempts during his career at Nebraska?

172. Which Nebraska fullback scored the most rushing touchdowns in his career?

163. Mike Rozier established the N.U. record, Big Eight record and NCAA standard when he averaged an unbelievable 7.156 yards per carry during his Husker career, 1981-83.

164. Gary Dixon, with a surprisingly small total of 508 yards, led the team in rushing during the regular season in 1972.

165. Mike Rozier holds not only the school record but also the Big Eight and NCAA records which he established in 1983 when he averaged an amazing 7.81 yards per carry.

166. Bobby Reynolds, the great Husker back, has the dubious distinction of losing the most yards. Reynolds lost 190 yards and gained 2386 yards.

167. In 11 of 12 seasons Solich has coached an all-conference running back. Only a gap in 1990 broke his streak.

168. Jerry Brown had 25 carries against Baylor in 1956 to establish the record.

169. Phillips recorded 100-plus games in each of the first 11 games. The streak was stopped at Oklahoma where he gained only 50 yards.

170. Rozier broke the record of Terry Miller of Oklahoma State who gained 4582 yards, 1974-77. Mike shattered that mark with 4780 yards gained, 1981-83.

171. The inimitable Mike Rozier proved to be a real workhorse for the team during his N.U. career, 1981-83, when he had a remarkable 668 rushing attempts.

172. Mark Schellen scored 12 rushing touchdowns during his Husker career, 1982-83. Tom Rathman matched that total during his Nebraska playing days, 1983-85.

173. Mike Rozier won a bushel of aw
Nebraska runner had the longest tou
mage. Who was this back?

174. When Mike Rozier broke the NCAA record for most rushing yards gained in four consecutive games, whose record did
he break?

175. Calvin Jones shared the team lead in receptions in 1992
with 14 catches. When was the last time a running back had
led the team in receiving?

176. Who was the first Husker running back to break 1000 yards
in a season after Bobby Reynolds did it in 1950?

177. Who had the most all-purpose running yards for Nebraska
in his career?

178. The same back was Nebraska's leading rusher in both 1974
and 1975. Who was he?

179. Which Husker fullback had the most rushing attempts in
one season?

180. Which school did Jarvis Redwine leave to come to
Nebraska?

181. Name the Husker running back who had the highest per
game rushing average during one season.

182. Until Rick Berns broke the single game rushing record
with 211 yards against Hawaii in 1976, an unlikely back had
held the record for 11 years. Who was he? What was the old
record?

ARTHUR
ANDERSEN

JR ANDERSEN & CO SC

Arthur Andersen LLP

33 West Monroe Street
Chicago IL 60603-5385
312 507 9802 Ext 33493 Voicemail
312 507 6748 Fax

173. Third string I-back Paul Miles scored on a 78 yard run against Kansas in November of 1983.

174. Rozier broke the record of Marcus Allen who had 926 yards in four games in 1981. Mike gained 929 yards in four games in 1983.

175. The last time a running back led the Husker team in receiving was in 1969 when Jeff Kinney caught 41 passes.

176. It was 21 years before another back reached the magic 1000 yard pinnacle. Jeff Kinney gained 1037 yards in 1971, the great national championship year.

177. The great Johnny Rodgers had 5586 yards during his N.U. career, 1970-72. He gained 745 yards rushing, 2479 yards in pass receptions, 1515 yards in punt returns and 847 yards in kickoff returns to set the school mark.

178. Monte Anthony gained 587 yards in 1974 and 722 yards in 1975 to lead the Huskers each season.

179. Dick Davis established the record with 162 attempts in 1967.

180. Redwine came to the Huskers by way of Oregon State. He was not happy with the way that the coaching staff at Oregon State had utilized him so he left and came to Nebraska.

181. None other than Mike Rozier holds the record. During his Heisman Trophy year of 1983 Rozier averaged 179.0 yards rushing per game over a punishing 12 game schedule.

182. Little 5-foot 8-inch Frank Solich established the rushing record with 204 yards against the Air Force in 1965. Solich always played football with the courage and heart of a giant.

183. Has Nebraska ever had two running backs gain over 1000 yards during one regular season?

184. Which Husker fullback gained the most rushing yards in his career?

185. In 1977 one N.U. player had the longest touchdown run and the longest run without a score. Who was this player?

186. Roger Craig, the great Husker I-back/fullback, had a brother who also played at Nebraska. What was his name and what position did he play?

187. Which N.U. player had the most rushing attempts in a career for a fullback?

188. In 1983 Mike Rozier tied an NCAA record for touchdowns scored in a season. How many did he score and whose record did he match?

189. In 1970 one N.U. ball carrier had the longest run for a score and the longest run with no score. Who was this player?

190. Who was the workhorse Nebraska running back who gained the tough yards in the 1978 Nebraska-Oklahoma game, Tom Osborne's first victory over Barry Switzer?

191. Which former walk-on set the Husker record for rushing yards gained in a season by a fullback?

192. When Mike Rozier set the NCAA record for highest gain per rush in his career (minimum of 500 rushes), whose record did he break? (Hint- he was an old N.U. nemesis.)

183. The "We-Backs" pair of Derek Brown and Calvin Jones accomplished this feat in 1992. Brown gained 1011 and Jones added 1210 yards.

184. Andra Franklin, the future Miami Dolphin, set the fullback standard with 1738 yards in his N.U. career, 1977-80.

185. The great I.M. Hipp ran 82 yards for a score against Kansas State and 73 yards and no score against Indiana.

186. Curtis Craig was a very talented wingback for Nebraska who lettered 1975-77.

187. Dick Davis set the record with 348 rushing attempts in his career, 1966-68.

188. Rozier scored 29 touchdowns in 1983 and tied Lydell Mitchell's record who scored 29 touchdowns for Penn State in 1971.

189. Joe Orduna ran 67 yards for a touchdown against Southern California and 41 yards without a score against Missouri.

190. Rick Berns scored once and gained 117 tough yards on 25 carries. He was named the ABC Offensive Player of the Game.

191. Tom Rathman not only established the rushing mark of 881 yards gained in 1985. He has gone on to a stellar career with the Super Bowl champion, San Francisco 49ers.

192. Billy Sims had the record of 7.087 yards per rush, 1975-79. Rozier broke that mark with a gain of 7.156 yards per rush, 1981-83.

193. Rick Berns broke the existing single game rushing record at N.U. in what year and against which team?

194. Which N.U. player had the longest run in N.U. football history that did not result in a touchdown?

195. Name the Husker I-back or halfback who had the most rushing attempts in one season.

196. Who had the most all-purpose running yards in one season for Nebraska?

197. Mike Rozier tied an NCAA record in 1983 for most games rushing for 100 yards or more in a season. How many such games did he have?

198. Who are the two Nebraska rushers to gain more than 2000 yards before the end of their sophomore seasons?

199. Which N.U. I-back or halfback recorded the most rushing attempts in one game and how many attempts were there?

200. Only once has an N.U. fullback gained over 200 yards rushing in one game. Who accomplished this feat and when?

201. Name the Husker player who gained the most rushing yards in one season by a fullback.

202. When Rick Berns set the single game rushing record in 1978 against Missouri, whose record did he break?

193. Berns gained 255 yards in 1978 against Missouri. Unfortunately, the Huskers had great difficulty stopping the Tigers and Missouri ended up on the winning end of the score, 35-31.

194. I.M. Hipp set the record against Indiana in 1977 when he had a 73 yard run that did not result in a score.

195. Mike Rozier, Heisman Trophy winner, had 275 in 1983.

196. Heisman Trophy winner Mike Rozier established the school record in 1983 with 2486 yards (2148 rushing, 232 kick-off returns, 106 pass receptions).

197. Rozier had 11 games with more than 100 yards rushing. Only Penn State, holding him to 71 yards in the opening game, kept Rozier from having the record all to himself.

198. The great Calvin Jones, 1991-1992, was the first Husker back to do this. He gained 1210 yards in his sophomore season to go with the 900 yards he gained as a freshman. Lawrence Phillips matched his feat with 508 yards in 1993 during his freshman season and a remarkable 1722 yards in his sophomore year of 1994, the Huskers' national championship season.

199. Rick Berns had 36 rushing attempts against Missouri in 1978. In that game Berns established a single game rushing record of 255 yards.

200. Little Frank Solich set a school record in rushing for 204 yards against Air Force in 1965.

201. Tom Rathman bulled his way for 881 yards in 1985.

202. Berns broke I.M. Hipp's record by one yard. Hipp had rushed for 254 yards against Indiana in 1977.

203. In 1971, for the greatest college team of all time, one player had the longest run without a touchdown and also the longest run for a score. Who was this player?

204. Why was there a close relationship between Mike Rozier and Irving Fryar?

205. In 1950 Bobby Reynolds set an NCAA record that stood for 38 years. What is the record?

206. As a sophomore Calvin Jones gained more yards rushing than how many Big Eight teams in 1992?

207. In which game did two Nebraska ball carriers first rush for more than 100 yards apiece in the same game?

208. How many touchdowns did Mike Rozier, who scored 49 in his career, tally against Oklahoma during his three years at Nebraska?

209. In Bobby Reynolds' phenomenal 1950 season, how many times did he score all of his team's points?

210. Has an N.U. running back ever gained more than 200 yards rushing against the Oklahoma Sooners in modern times?

211. Which Husker running back gained the most rushing yards in one season?

203. Bill Olds ran 58 yards against Iowa State and also 67 yards for a touchdown against Texas A&M.

204. The two had a lot in common. They lived close together in New Jersey. Rozier's grandmother lived across the street from Fryar's parents and both fathers worked at the same company.

205. Reynolds scored at an average of 17.4 points per game—157 points in 9 games. That remarkable record was secure until the great Barry Sanders from Oklahoma State broke it in 1988.

206. By himself Calvin Jones gained more rushing yards (1210) than four entire Big Eight teams—Kansas State, Oklahoma State, Colorado and Missouri.

207. Tony Davis and John O'Leary accomplished this feat against Kansas State on November 17, 1973. Davis gained 111 yards on 21 carries and O'Leary added 100 yards more on 17 carries.

208. Amazingly, Rozier was only able to score one touchdown against the Sooners, that coming in the 1983 game, his last regular season contest in his Husker career.

209. Bobby accomplished this amazing feat three times in his great sophomore season of 1950.

210. Surprisingly, this feat has been accomplished only once, in 1983, when Mike Rozier pounded the Sooners for 205 yards in Nebraska's 28-21 victory.

211. Mike Rozier rushed for an unbelievable 2148 yards in 1983 to set the Husker record.

212. Of the following running backs, which are from Nebraska?—Mike Rozier, Jeff Smith, Andra Franklin, Roger Craig, I.M. Hipp, Jarvis Redwine.

213. Who had the most all-purpose running yards in one game for N.U.?

214. What was Calvin Jones' longest run from scrimmage during his Husker career?

215. Name the Nebraska running back who had the most rushing attempts in one season.

216. In 1982, when Mike Rozier set the N.U. single season rushing record, whose record did he break?

217. When Mike Rozier broke the NCAA record for most rushing touchdowns in a season, with 29, whose record did he break?

218. In 1969, when Joe Orduna went down for the season with a knee injury, which future star filled in with great success?

219. When Mike Rozier set the school record for rushing touchdowns in a career, whose record did he break?

220. Mike Rozier gained a Big Eight record 2148 yards rushing in 1983. Whose record did he break?

221. When Mike Rozier broke the career record for scoring at Nebraska, whose record did he break?

212. None of these fine Husker running backs can claim to be from this great state. They were all imports from other parts of the country.

213. Calvin Jones set the school mark in 1991 when he had 298 all-purpose yards against Kansas. Jones had 294 rushing yards rushing and 4 yards receiving in the game.

214. Calvin scored on a 90 yard run against Oklahoma State in 1992. His run was also the longest of the year by a Nebraska player.

215. Mike Rozier established the school record with an amazing 275 carries in 1983.

216. Rozier, with 1689 yards, smashed the old record of Bobby Reynolds who had 1342 yards in 1950.

217. Rozier broke the record of Lydell Mitchell who scored 26 touchdowns for Penn State in 1971.

218. Jeff Kinney was given his big chance and he responded by being named the Big Eight Sophomore Back of the Year in 1969.

219. Rozier shattered the record of Rick Berns who had 30 rushing touchdowns in his Husker career, 1976-78.

220. The old record holder was Ernest Anderson of Oklahoma State who had set the record a year earlier in 1982 with 1877 yards.

221. Rozier broke Johnny Rodger's record of 270 points tallied in his career at Nebraska, 1970-72.

222. Who was the last rusher to lead the Husker team in rushing with less than a 1000 yards gained in a season?

223. In 1967, when Dick Davis set the N.U. fullback record for rushing yards gained in a season, whose record did he eclipse?

224. In 1983. when Mike Rozier set the single game rushing record at N.U., whose record did he shatter?

225. Which former Nebraska back was the first NFL player to gain more than 1000 rushing and receiving in a single season?

226. In 1983, when Mike Rozier broke the season record for rushing touchdowns, whose record did he break?

227. Amazingly, Nebraska had the top two rushers in the Big Eight in 1992. Who were they and who ranked first in the conference?

222. In 1990 Leodis Flowers led the team in rushing and gained 940 yards.

223. Davis broke the rushing record of Jerry Brown who had gained 690 yards in 1956.

224. Rozier captured the record that he wanted very badly, rushing for 285 yards against Kansas and shattering the mark of 255 yards set by Rick Berns against Missouri in 1978.

225. Roger Craig accomplished this incredible feat of skill and endurance as a member of the San Francisco 49ers. In 1985 Craig had 1050 yards rushing and 1016 yards receiving.

226. Rozier, who scored 29 rushing touchdowns in 1983, broke the record of 20 scored by Bobby Reynolds in his great sophomore season of 1950.

227. Calvin Jones gained 1210 yards to lead the conference and his "We Back" counterpart, Derek Brown, chipped in with 1011 yards.

Calvin Jones

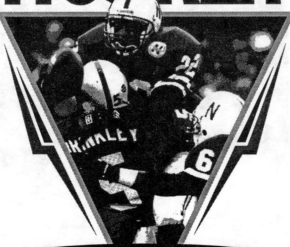

RECEIVERS

4

228. On what charge was Johnny Rodgers arrested in the spring of 1971, a charge that threatened to destroy his future in football?

229. Which N.U. player established the single game record for most pass receptions by a tight end? How many?

230. Two players hold the record for most touchdown receptions in a season by a split end. Who are the players and how many scoring tosses did they gather in?

231. Which N.U. player set the school record for touchdown receptions in a career by a wingback? How many scores?

232. Which Nebraska player established the freshman record for number of passes caught in a season? How many?

233. Which Husker player had the most pass receptions in one game? How many?

234. Which Nebraska player set the record for most touchdown receptions in a career by a split end? How many scores?

235. Name the N.U. player who set the school record for most pass receptions in one game by a wingback. How many catches?

236. What is unique about tight end Matt Shaw's career at Nebraska?

237. Which N.U. player set the record for pass receptions in a season by a tight end? How many?

238. Name the Husker player who had the most pass receptions in his career. How many?

228. He was charged with participating in the armed robbery of a gas station when he was a freshman at Nebraska. He overcame the bad publicity and won the Heisman Trophy in 1972 by his football exploits.

229. Jim McFarland set the mark with 7 pass receptions against Texas A&M in 1969.

230. Guy Ingles in 1970 and Frosty Anderson in 1973 both had 8 touchdown receptions to set the school record.

231. Who else but Johnny Rodgers could haul in 26 touchdown receptions in his career at Nebraska, 1970-72.

232. Rocke Loken set the yearling record in 1973 when he had 19 pass receptions during the season.

233. Dennis Richnafsky established a lofty mark when he had an astounding 14 receptions against Kansas State in 1967.

234. Jon Bostick hauled in 15 touchdown passes in his career at N.U., 1989-91, to establish the school record.

235. Johnny Rodgers established the school mark by hauling in 10 passes against Kansas State in 1971.

236. Though he was the team's No.1 tight end in 1994, Shaw played in 33 varsity games for the Huskers without making one pass reception in a game.

237. Johnny Mitchell, most recently of the New York Jets, set the single season mark with 31 pass receptions in 1991.

238. To no one's surprise, the answer is the one-and-only Johnny Rodgers. He had 143 pass receptions in his illustrious N.U. career, 1970-72.

239. Which Nebraska receiver had the highest average gain per pass reception in his career?

240. Gerald Armstrong, N.U. tight end, tied an NCAA record in 1992. What was the amazing record that he tied?

241. Which Husker player holds the record for most pass receptions in a career by a tight end? How many?

242. Name the N.U. player who set the record for yardage gained via pass receptions in one game by a wingback.

243. Which Omaha high school did Johnny Rodgers attend?

244. Name the Husker player who established the school mark for most yardage gained by pass receptions in one game by a split end.

245. Which Husker player set the school record for most pass receptions in one season by a wingback? How many?

246. Which Nebraska player had the most yards in pass receptions in one game?

247. Johnny Rodgers was drafted by the San Diego Chargers in 1973. Did he sign with them that year?

239. Surprisingly, the answer is not Johnny Rodgers. Rob Schnitzler had a average of 21.60 yards gained per catch during his career, 1984-86, on 30 receptions for 648 yards.

240. Armstrong went six-for-six on receptions for touchdowns before he caught a pass that did not produce a score. Armstrong didn't catch many passes but he really made them count.

241. Jerry List established the record with 64 pass receptions in his N.U. career, 1970-72.

242. Irving Fryar established the mark with 138 yards gained in the 84-13 blowout of Minnesota in 1983.

243. Johnny Rodgers was a star at Omaha Technical High and showed flashes of the brilliance that would win him the Heisman Trophy at Nebraska in 1972.

244. Chuck Malito set the record with an amazing 166 yards against Hawaii in 1976.

245. The great Johnny Rodgers established the school mark with 55 pass receptions in 1972.

246. Chuck Malito gained 166 yards in receptions against a badly out-manned Hawaii team in 1976, a game which resulted in a 68-3 blowout by the Huskers.

247. Rodgers opted not to sign with the NFL team and went instead to play for the Montreal Alouettes of the Canadian Football League. He played in Canada, 1973-76, and then signed with and played for the Chargers in 1977 and 1978.

248. Name the Husker player who set the school record for most pass reception yardage in one game by a tight end.

249. Name the Husker player who set the school record for yardage gained by pass receptions in one season by a wingback.

250. Which Nebraska receiver had the most touchdown receptions in one season? How many?

251. Which Nebraska receiver had the highest average gain per pass reception in one season?

252. Name the N.U. Player who had the most pass receptions in one season. How many passes did he catch?

253. In what season did an N.U. player first have three touchdown receptions in one game?

254. Can you name the player who set the record for most touchdown receptions in one game by a split end?

255. Which N.U. player holds the record for most pass reception yardage in a career by a tight end?

256. Name the Husker player who had the most yards gained in pass receptions in his career.

257. Which N.U. receiver had the most touchdown receptions in his career as a Husker? How many?

248. Johnny Mitchell established the mark when he had an outstanding day against Oklahoma in 1991. In that game Mitchell had 137 yards in pass receptions.

249. The one and only Johnny Rodgers set the record with 942 yards gained in 1972.

250. The great Johnny Rodgers set the school record with 11 TD receptions in 1971.

251. Johnny Mitchell had a amazing average of 25.64 yards per catch in 1990 on 11 receptions for 282 yards.

252. Johnny Rodgers, the Heisman Trophy winner, set the school mark when he hauled in 55 passes in 1972.

253. Clarence Swanson was the first player to accomplish this feat when he did it against Colorado State in 1921.

254. The player happens to be the colorful Frosty Anderson who gathered in 3 TD passes against Minnesota in 1973, in Tom Osborne's first season as head coach.

255. The inimitable Junior Miller holds the school record with 1045 yards in pass receptions during his Husker career, 1977-79.

256. The incomparable Johnny Rodgers set the record with 2479 yards gained on 143 receptions during his Husker career, 1970-72.

257. Johnny Rodgers, the Great One, hauled in 26 touchdown receptions in his outstanding Husker career, 1970-72.

258. Name the Nebraska player who established the record for most touchdown receptions in a season by a tight end. How many?

259. Who was the last Husker to have more than 30 pass receptions in a season?

260. Which N.U. player holds the school record for most pass receptions in a career by a wingback?

261. Name the N.U. receiver who scored on the longest touchdown pass in Nebraska football history. How long was the reception?

262. Which player holds the record for most pass receptions in one game by a Nebraska split end? How many receptions?

263. Which N.U. player had the most yards gained in pass receptions in one season?

264. Name the Husker player who holds the school record for most touchdown receptions in a career by a tight end. How many?

265. Which player established the school mark for yardage gained via pass receptions in a career by a wingback?

266. Which player holds the N.U. record for most pass receptions in a career by a split end?

267. Name the Husker player who holds the record for most pass reception yardage in a season by a tight end.

268. Name the Nebraska player who established the school record for most yardage gained via pass receptions in a career by a split end.

258. Junior Miller tallied 7 TD receptions in 1979 to set the record for tight ends. This was later tied by Todd Millikan in 1988, Johnny Mitchell in 1990 and Gerald Armstrong in 1992.

259. All-American Johnny Mitchell hauled in 31 passes in 1991, the first time a player had more than 30 receptions since the great Irving Fryar had 40 in 1983.

260. Johnny Rodgers established the record with 143 pass receptions in his Husker career, 1970-72.

261. End Freeman White hooked up with Fred Duda to record a 95 yard touchdown reception against Colorado in 1965.

262. Dennis Richnafsky set the mark against Kansas State in 1967 with 14 receptions.

263. The record belongs to Johnny Rodgers who gained 942 yards on 55 receptions in 1972, his senior year as a Husker.

264. Todd Millikan owns this record with 14 TD receptions in his great Husker career, 1985-88.

265. None other than Johnny Rodgers set the mark with 2479 yards in his incomparable career, 1970-72.

266. Guy Ingles, the small target, set a large record by pulling in 74 pass receptions in his career at Nebraska, 1968-70.

267. Junior Miller set the record with his outstanding year in 1978. During that remarkable season he had 609 yards in pass receptions.

268. Guy Ingles, the Little Big Man, gained 1157 yards in pass receptions during his Husker career, 1968-70.

269. Nebraska players have led the league in receptions per game only twice in modern times. When did this take place and who were the players?

270. Which player had the most touchdown receptions in one season by a wingback? How many scores?

271. Name the player who holds the school mark for most pass receptions in a season by a split end. How many catches did he make?

272. Which Husker player had the most touchdown receptions in one game by a wingback? How many scores?

273. Who holds the school record for most yardage gained via pass receptions in one season by a split end?

274. When Johnny Rodgers set the career record for number of pass receptions, whose record did he break?

275. In 1976, when Chuck Malito set the season reception yardage record for a split end, whose record did he break?

276. When Johnny Rodgers broke the career record for yardage gained by pass receptions, whose mark did he eclipse?

277. Which Husker tight end later became a Nebraska state senator?

269. Johnny Rodgers led the league in 1971 with 4.4 receptions per game and Tim Smith led with 2.7 receptions per game in 1979.

270. Johnny Rodgers established the record for a wingback with 11 touchdown receptions in 1971.

271. Dennis Richnafsky established the mark of 36 pass receptions in 1967, his last year at Nebraska and the first of N.U.'s two consecutive 6-4-0 seasons.

272. Johnny Rodgers hauled in 3 touchdown passes against Minnesota in 1971 to establish the record.

273. Chuck Malito is the record holder with 615 yards gained in 1976.

274. Amazingly, Johnny broke Jeff Kinney's pass reception record. Kinney had recorded 81 pass receptions in his illustrious career at Nebraska.

275. The previous record holder was Guy Ingles whose 603 yards gained in 1970 was surpassed by the 615 yards gained by Malito.

276. The former record holder was Guy Ingles who had 1157 yards gained on 74 receptions in his N.U. career, 1968-70.

277. Jim McFarland, after a successful pro career with the St. Louis Cardinals and the Miami Dolphins, was appointed to the Nebraska Legislature in 1986.

Irving Fryar

5

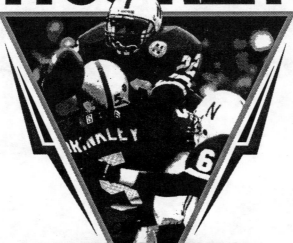

HUSKER TRIVIA

KICKERS AND KICK RETURNERS

278. Which Nebraska place kicker had the longest field goal in school history? How long was the kick?

279. Name the N.U. place kicker who had the most consecutive successful extra point conversions.

280. Which Husker place kicker had the highest field goal success percentage in his career? (minimum of 10 attempts)

281. Name the Nebraska punter who had the most punts in his career.

282. Who had the most punt returns for touchdowns in his career at Nebraska? How many scores?

283. Who had the highest kickoff return average for a season at Nebraska?

284. Name the Nebraska place kicker who had the highest field goal success percentage in one season (minimum of 5 attempts).

285. What was the longest Husker kickoff return in school football history and who was the player who made it?

286. Which N.U. place kicker had the most consecutive field goals?

287. Which Nebraska place kicker had the highest extra point conversion percentage in his career?

278. Paul Rogers had a mammoth field goal against Kansas in 1969. The kick measured 55 yards. Rogers' feat was later matched by Billy Todd with his own 55 yarder against Kansas in 1977 and Chris Drennan against Northern Illinois in 1989.

279. Gregg Barrios had an incredible string of 83 PATs without a miss beginning on October 19, 1986 and ending on September 8, 1990.

280. Dean Sukup in his Husker career (lettered 1977-79) made 12 of 16 field goal attempts. That converts to a .750 percentage mark.

281. Mike Stigge, a four-year regular, had 167 punts in his Husker career, 1989-1992.

282. Heisman Trophy winner Johnny Rodgers had a remarkable 7 touchdowns from punt returns in his Husker career, 1970-72.

283. Pat Fischer established the Nebraska school record in 1958 with a 33.7 yard average on 7 kickoff returns.

284. Eddie Neil established the school mark by making 8 of 9 field goal attempts in 1981. That converts to a .889 percentage mark.

285. The Husker record is an incredible return of 105 yards by Owen Frank in 1911 against Kansas State. It is one record that may never be broken at Nebraska.

286. Dale Klein kicked 9 consecutive field goals in the 1985 season.

287. Gregg Barrios missed only 2 PATs out of 129 attempts for a .984 percentage mark, 1986-1990.

288. When was the last time the Huskers gave up a kickoff return for a touchdown?

289. Which Husker player had the most punt returns for touchdowns in one season? How many scores?

290. Who was the N.U. player that gained the most kickoff return yards in his career?

291. Who had the most field goals in his career as a place kicker at Nebraska? How many?

292. Name the Nebraska player who had the highest punt return average in his career.

293. Why is it likely that Darin Erstad won't return in the 1995 season to punt for Nebraska?

294. Name the place kicker who had the highest extra point conversion percentage in one season.

295. Who had the highest punt return average for one season at Nebraska?

296. Who returned the most kickoffs in his career at Nebraska? How many?

297. Which Husker place kicker had the most field goals in one season? How many?

298. Which Nebraska player set the school record for punting average in his career?

288. The last time this happened was in 1978 when Howard Ballage from Colorado ran back a kickoff 100 yards for a touchdown.

289. Johnny Rodgers had three touchdowns on punt returns in 1971.

290. Tyrone Hughes gained 1443 yards in kickoff returns during his Husker career 1989-1992.

291. Dale Klein kicked 27 field goals in his Husker career, 1984-86 to set the record.

292. Johnny Rodgers established the school record with a 15.5 yard average for 98 punt returns in his Heisman career at Nebraska.

293. He will probably not return to the team because he is the top college baseball prospect.

294. Kevin Seibel converted 43 of 44 extra point opportunities in 1981 for a .977 percentage mark.

295. Rod Smith set the mark with an 18.9 yard average in 1986 on 12 punt returns.

296. Tyrone Hughes smashed the previous record with 61 kickoff returns during his illustrious Husker career, 1989-92. He is the best Nebraska has ever had at this duty.

297. Gregg Barrios set the standard with 14 field goals during his finest Husker season, 1990.

298. Mike Stigge broke Jack Pesek's 45 year old record by averaging 41.75 yards per punt during his career, 1989-92.

299. Who was Nebraska's only modern era 4-year starting punter?

300. Who returned the most kickoffs in one season at Nebraska? How many?

301. Who had the most punt return yards in his career at Nebraska?

302. Which N.U. placekicker had the most extra point conversions in his career?

303. Name the Husker player who had the most punt return yards in one season.

304. Which N.U. punter had the most punts in a season? How many?

305. Who gained the most kickoff return yards in one season for Nebraska?

306. Which N.U. place kicker had the most extra point conversions in one season?

307. Name the Husker player who had the most punt return yards in one game.

308. Who is Nebraska's single season record holder for punting average?

299. Mike Stigge was a mainstay at the position, 1989-92, and finished his N.U. career with school records for punts, punting yards and career average.

300. Dana Brinson returned 23 kickoffs in 1988 for a total of 510 yards to set the single season record.

301. Johnny Rodgers set a record that may never be broken at Nebraska. He had 1515 yards in punt returns during his illustrious Husker career, 1970-72.

302. Kevin Seibel converted 151 of 156 PAT attempts during his career, 1979-82, to establish the record.

303. Johnny Rodgers had 618 yards in punt returns in 1972, his senior year at Nebraska.

304. Dana Stephenson had an incredible 69 punts in 1967 to set the school record. He averaged 35.1 yards per punt. Interestingly, he was also the team's leading punt returner with a 7.1 yard average on 28 returns.

305. Nebraska's greatest kickoff return man, Tyrone Hughes, returned 18 kickoffs for 523 yards in 1990.

306. Rich Sanger established the school mark with 60 PATs in 1971, the year of the greatest college team of all time.

307. Johnny Rodgers, one of the greatest kick returners in the history of college football, established the school mark with an unbelievable 170 yards in punt returns against Oklahoma State in 1971, including a school record 92 yarder.

308. Grant Campbell set the record in 1981 with a 43.4 yard average per punt.

309. Which place kicker had the most extra point conversions in one game for Nebraska?

310. Which N.U. player had the most punt returns in a single season? How many?

311. On October 6, 1991 Tyrone Hughes, Nebraska's great return man, tied an NCAA record against Kansas State. What is the record that he matched?

312. Name the player who had the longest punt return for Nebraska. How long was the return?

313. Who is Nebraska's all-time leading kick scorer?

314. Which N.U. place kicker has kicked the most field goals during his career as a Husker?

315. Name the Nebraska place kicker who scored the most points by kicking in a season.

309. Owen Frank registered an astounding 17 extra point conversions against the Haskell Indians in 1910, a game that the Huskers won by a score of 119-0.

310. Johnny Rodgers returned 39 punts in 1972 to set the school mark.

311. Hughes had a truly remarkable day against the Wildcats. He tied the record for most total return yards in a game. Hughes gained 247 return yards on eight punt and kickoff returns.

312. The one and only Johnny Rodgers had an incredible return of 92 yards against Oklahoma State in the golden 1971 season.

313. Gregg Barrios converted 127 of 129 extra points and 26 of 35 field goals for 205 points during his career at N.U. which ended in 1990.

314. Dale Klein, during his player career, which ended in 1986, converted 27 of 41 field goal attempts to set the record.

315. Gregg Barrios scored 87 points in 1990 to set the single season record at Nebraska.

Johnny Rodgers

6

HUSKER

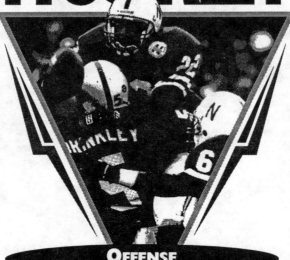

TRIVIA

HUSKER

OFFENSE

316. A Devaney-coached Husker team gained more than 400 yards rushing only twice. When did this take place?

317. What was the most points scored by Nebraska at Memorial Stadium?

318. What the longest scoring run by an N.U. offensive lineman?

319. Under Tom Osborne's guidance, how many NCAA rushing titles have the Huskers claimed?

320. Which N.U. player scored the most points in his career?

321. In which game did Nebraska first use the Fumbleroosky?

322. Nebraska set an NCAA record for most first downs made in one game. When did they set the record and against whom did they accomplish this feat?

323. Under Tom Osborne's leadership has Nebraska ever lost a game in which the team has rushed for 400 or more yards?

324. Which Nebraska player scored the most points in one game in N.U. football history?

316. In 1965 the Huskers gained 419 yards rushing against Kansas and in 1971 Nebraska gained 411 rushing against old reliable Kansas.

317. The Huskers scored 77 points against Arizona State in 1995.

318. Dean Steinkuhler ran the Fumbleroosky play against Miami in the 1984 Orange Bowl. he gained 19 yards and scored Nebraska's first touchdown in a 31-30 loss to the Hurricanes.

319. Through 1994, in Osborne's 22 years at Nebraska, the Huskers have won nine national rushing titles.

320. Mike Rozier set the mark with an awesome 312 points scored in his illustrious Husker career, 1981-83.

321. Against Oklahoma in 1979 this intentional fumble play was tried. Randy Schleusner picked up Jeff Quinn's fumble and scored from the 15 yard line. Unfortunately, Oklahoma won the game 17-14 with Billy Sims shredding the Husker defense for 247 yards rushing.

322. The Huskers made 44 first downs against New Mexico State on September 18, 1982. Nebraska won the game by a score of 68-0.

323. No, the Huskers have a perfect 71-0 record in the Osborne era when they have reached the 400-yard rushing mark.

324. Calvin Jones broke an 81 year old record when he tallied 36 points on six touchdowns against Kansas on November 9, 1991.

325. What are the most points an N.U. team has scored in one game in the Devaney-Osborne era?

326. What is the greatest number of pass attempts made by a Husker team in one game?

327. How many games in a row has Nebraska won when rushing for 300 yards or more?

328. In 1983 Nebraska set a Big Eight record for the greatest number of points scored in one half. Against which team was the record set and how many points did Nebraska score in the half?

329. Name the Husker player who scored the most points in one season.

330. How many sacks did Outland Trophy winner Zach Wiegert allow in three years as a starter?

331. In what year did Nebraska switch to the triple option as their basic offensive philosophy?

332. Which N.U. player produced the most yards in total offense in a season?

325. The annihilation of the Minnesota Gophers by 84-13 in 1983 was the high water mark of N.U. scoring in the A.D. period (after Devaney). In fact, it was the most points scored by Nebraska since the 100-0 execution of Nebraska Wesleyan in 1917.

326. The record for pass attempts is 42 which was set against Iowa State in 1972, a game which ended in a 23-23 tie.

327. The Huskers have won 61 straight games in which they have stopped the 300 yard rushing mark. Their last loss was to Michigan in the 1986 Sunkist Fiesta Bowl when they rushed for 304 yards and were outscored 27-23.

328. Nebraska set the scoring record against Colorado when the unbelievable Husker offense tallied 55 points in the 2nd half of the game and 48 points in the 3rd quarter alone. The 48 points in a quarter broke the old record of 25 also set by Nebraska in 1978 against Kansas. The Colorado game ended in a 69-19 N.U. victory.

329. Mike Rozier tallied an incredible 174 points on 29 touchdowns in 1983 to establish the N.U. record.

330. Amazingly, he allowed only one sack in three years. In 1994 he was not called for a single holding penalty.

331. This change took place prior to the 1980 season. Since switching, the Huskers have won nine of a possible 15 Big Eight championships and lead the conference in 11 of 12 offensive categories.

332. The great Jerry Tagge had the remarkable total of 2333 yards of total offense in 1971. He had 314 yards rushing and 2019 yards passing during that fantastic season.

333. Nebraska set an NCAA single game record for rushing first downs. when did the Huskers set this record and against whom did they establish the mark?

334. Which N.U. player scored the most touchdowns in one game?

335. Nebraska is known as a rushing powerhouse in the Big Eight Conference. Which team has led the conference in touchdown passes since 1980?

336. The Huskers ran the Fumbleroosky for the first time in 1979. When was the next time the play was used by Nebraska?

337. What is the most points scored by Nebraska in one game?

338. In the Devaney-Osborne era, when did the Huskers first gain more than 600 yards in total offense in one game?

339. In 1992 the Huskers set a school record for most consecutive quarters without a turnover. How many quarters did they play without giving the ball away?

340. Against which team did Nebraska record the most yards in total offense in a game?

341. What was the greatest combined score in an N.U. Big Eight game?

333. The Huskers made 36 rushing first downs against New Mexico State on September 18, 1982. The result was a 68-0 Nebraska blowout.

334. Three players hold the school record for touchdowns in one game. Bill Chaloupka scored 6 against Doane in 1907 and Harvey Rathbone also scored 6 gains Peru Teachers in 1910 and also against the Haskell Indians in 1910. Eighty-one years later Calvin Jones tallied 6 touchdowns against Kansas in 1991.

335. Amazingly, Nebraska also leads in this category. Since 1980 Nebraska has scored 213 touchdowns through the air. Missouri ranks a distant second and their won-loss record is abysmal.

336. In the 1984 Orange Bowl, Dean Steinkuhler ran the ball 19 yards for the Husker's first touchdown against Miami of Florida, in a game Nebraska eventually lost 31-30. In both instances the Fumbleroosky produced a touchdown.

337. Unbelievably, the Huskers scored 119 points against the Haskell Indians in 1910. The final score was 119-0.

338. The first occurred in 1971 when the Huskers gained 603 yards against the Missouri Tigers.

339. Nebraska played an amazing 24 quarters, or six games, without a turnover enroute to a school record low 12 turnovers for the season.

340. New Mexico State gave up an incredible 883 yards of total offense in 1982.

341. The record was established in the 1983 Iowa State game in which 101 points were scored, 72 by the Huskers and 29 by the Cyclones.

342. Of the top ten games in terms of total offense for N.U., only one took place before 1980. When was that game?

343. Who was the first player to lead the Big Eight Conference in scoring as both a freshman and a sophomore?

344. In 1935 an N.U. player was the conference leader in scoring. Who was he and how many points did he score?

345. Name the player who scored the most touchdowns in one season for the Huskers.

346. Against which team did Nebraska record the most rushing yards in one game?

347. Continuing the Husker's futility in bowl games, Miami shut out and completely dominated Nebraska 22-0 in the 1992 Federal Express Orange Bowl. How many games had it been since the Huskers had last been shut out?

348. In 1936 an N.U. player was the conference scoring leader. Who was he and how many points did he score?

349. The top three passing performances for the Huskers occurred in the same season. During which year did this happen?

350. Which Nebraska player scored the most touchdowns in his career?

351. What is the Husker record for points scored in the first quarter of a game?

352. In 1950 an N.U. player was the conference scoring leader. Who was this player and how many points did he score?

342. In 1978 the Huskers gained 799 yards against Kansas.

343. Calvin Jones holds this record with an 8.4 points per game pace in 1991 and 8.2 per game average in 1992.

344. Sam Francis led the league with 29 points scored in 1935.

345. Mike Rozier, in his Heisman season of 1983, tallied an extraordinary total of 29 touchdowns.

346. New Mexico State gave up an impressive 677 yards rushing to the Huskers in 1982.

347. This was Nebraska's first shutout in almost twenty years. It had last happened in Osborne's first season as head coach when Oklahoma crushed the Huskers 27-0 in 1973, 220 games earlier.

348. Lloyd Cardwell led the conference with 36 points scored in 1936.

349. The Husker's banner passing year was in 1972 when they gained 360 yards against Kansas, 338 yards against Oklahoma State and 329 yards against Missouri.

350. Mike Rozier scored an incredible total of 52 touchdowns in his career as a Husker, 1981-83.

351. Talk about fast starts!! The Huskers scored 35 points in the first quarter of the October 15, 1988 game against Oklahoma State. The 7th ranked Huskers went on to demolish the 10th ranked Cowboys 63-42 in Lincoln.

352. The great Bobby Reynolds, in his superlative year of 1950, led the conference in scoring with 157 points.

353. Nebraska set an NCAA record for total offense in one game, a record that was later broken. Against whom did the Huskers set the record and when?

354. Has Nebraska ever averaged more than 225 yards a game passing in a season?

355. What is the fewest touchdown passes that Nebraska has thrown in a season during modern times?

356. In 1964 an N.U. player led the Big Eight conference in scoring. Who was this player and how many points did he score?

357. Which player produced the most yards in total offense in a single game for Nebraska?

358. What was the highest number of points scored in a season by a Devaney-coached Nebraska team?

359. What is the fewest yards rushing that the Huskers have gained in a game?

360. Who is the all-time leading scorer at Nebraska over the course of a career?

361. In 1970 an N.U. player led the Big Eight conference in scoring. Who was this player and how many points did he score?

353. The Huskers gained a remarkable 883 yards against hapless New Mexico State in 1982. Houston now holds the record with 1021 yards gained against S.M.U. in 1989.

354. No, surprisingly Nebraska has never averaged more than 221 yards per game passing, a mark established in 1972 with Dave Humm at the throttle.

355. Unbelievably the Huskers only had one touchdown pass during the entire 1959 season and the 1960 season. Not surprisingly, Nebraska didn't win many games during either of those seasons.

356. Kent McCloughan led the conference in scoring with 74 points in 1964.

357. Jerry Tagge set the mark with a 319 yard performance against Missouri in 1971, as part of the greatest college team of all time. In that game he had 85 yards rushing and 234 yards passing.

358. The great national champion team of 1971 scored 507 points, including the Orange Bowl victory over Alabama.

359. How things have changed! The Huskers were only able to gain 15 measly yards rushing against Penn State on October 15, 1949. Not surprisingly, Nebraska lost the game 22-7.

360. Mike Rozier established a scoring mark at N.U. which may not be broken for many years. During his playing career, 1981-83, he tallied 312 points to eclipse the mark of Johnny Rodgers who scored 270 points.

361. Joe Orduna led the conference in scoring in 1970 with 92 points.

362. Which Nebraska player produced the most yards in total offense during his playing career?

363. Who are the only two Nebraska players to gain more than 2000 yards in a season in all-purpose yards?

364. In 1972 an N.U. player led the Big Eight conference in scoring. Who was this player and how many points did he score?

365. Who holds the N.U. freshman record for total offense in a season?

366. Who is the only non-quarterback on the top ten list of single-game total offense leaders at Nebraska?

367. Nebraska established an NCAA record for number of points scored in a season. How many points did the Huskers score and during which season was the record set?

368. How many times since 1950 has Nebraska passed for more than 300 yards in one game?

369. An N.U. player was the Big Eight conference scoring leader in 1982. Who was he and how many points did he score?

370. When did Bob Devaney decide to change Nebraska's offensive scheme to the I-formation?

371. Has Nebraska ever averaged more than 400 yards rushing per game in a season?

362. Jerry Tagge, the Green Bay great, finished his Husker career with 5283 yards in total offense. Tagge had 579 yards rushing and 4704 yards passing.

363. Only the great Johnny Rodgers, with 2011 yards in 1972, and the equally great Mike Rozier, with 2486 yards in 1983, have cracked the 2000 yard plateau in all-purpose yards.

364. Johnny Rodgers led the conference in scoring in 1972 with 102 points.

365. Turner Gill established the yearling total offense record in 1980 with 979 yards.

366. Calvin Jones, in his record setting performance against Kansas on November 9, 1991, gained 294 yards rushing to place him 6th on the all-time list.

367. In 1983 Nebraska scored a phenomenal 624 points in 12 games to shatter the old record of 560 points by Brigham Young in 12 games in 1980.

368. Surprisingly, the Huskers have accomplished this feat only four times. They gained 360 against Kansas in 1972, 338 against Oklahoma State in 1972, 329 yards against Missouri in 1972 and 314 yards against Utah in 1968.

369. Mike Rozier led the conference in scoring in 1982 with 102 points.

370. The switch took place in 1969 and Nebraska's football fortunes have been bright ever since.

371. Yes, this has occurred once. In 1983 the Huskers averaged 401.7 yards rushing over 12 regular season games.

372. When did Nebraska first use the Bounceroosky?

373. What is Nebraska's record for consecutive games scored in?

374. The 1983 team established an NCAA record for most yards gained in a season. How many yards did the Huskers gain?

375. When did Nebraska first use the Bummeroosky?

376. In 1983 Nebraska ranked first nationally in scoring and rushing offense but second in total offense. Which team was first in total offense?

377. Which Husker player established the freshman season scoring record?

378. When the Huskers scored 76 points against West Texas in 1993 how long had it been since Nebraska had scored that many points?

379. What was the greatest combined score in an N.U. game?

380. What is Nebraska's record for most consecutive games being shut out?

372. The Huskers used this trick play against the Oklahoma Sooners in the 1982 shootout. Turner Gill bounced a long lateral to Irving Fryar who then passed 37 yards to tight end Mitch Krenk. N.U. went on to win the game 28-24.

373. The Huskers scored in 220 straight games, from the 1974 Cotton Bowl to the 1992 Orange Bowl, a 22-0 shutout at the hands of Miami of Florida.

374. The "Scoring Explosion" erupted for 6560 total yards gained in 12 games in 1983.

375. The Huskers first pulled this fake punt play against Missouri on November 1, 1975. N.U. was leading 10-7 in the second quarter. After John O'Leary scored from the 40 on the fake, the Huskers went on to bury the Tigers 30-7.

376. Pass-happy Brigham Young was first in total offense and naturally they were also first in passing offense. The Cougars averaged 584.2 yards a game in total offense and 381.2 yards a game in passing offense.

377. Will Curtis set the yearling scoring record in 1981 by tallying 48 points.

378. It had been 10 years since so many points had been tallied. The "Scoring Explosion" rang up 84 points in the 84-13 execution of Minnesota in 1983.

379. The largest combined score was an incredible 133 points which was set in a 102-31 victory over Creighton University in 1905.

380. The Huskers were shut out in 4 consecutive games, the last 3 of the 1942 season and the first game of the 1943 season.

381. Two Husker players established an NCAA record for number of touchdowns and points scored by two players from the same team during one season. Name these two players.

382. What was the most points Nebraska has scored in a single game against a Big Eight opponent?

383. Against which team did Nebraska set its all-time single game passing record?

384. In a recent game the Huskers actually gained only 179 yards in total offense and yet won the game by two touchdowns. Who was the unlikely victim?

385. Nebraska set an NCAA record for net rushing yards in one game. When did they accomplish this and against whom was the record set?

386. The great 1983 team established an NCAA record for touchdowns scored in a season. How many did they score?

381. Mike Rozier and Turner Gill set the mark in 1983 with 40 touchdowns and 240 points. Barry Sanders and Hart Lee Dykes of Oklahoma State now own the record with 54 scores and 324 points, established in 1988.

382. The Huskers scored 72 points against Iowa State in 1983 to set the scoring mark.

383. Kansas gave up 360 yards passing to the Huskers in 1972.

384. The Huskers beat the Oklahoma Sooners in 1993, 21-7, with such a paltry offensive output, mainly on the basis of turnovers, field position and solid defense.

385. The Huskers rushed for an unbelievable total of 677 yards against New Mexico State in 1982. The visitors from New Mexico were annihilated by a score of 68-0. This record was later eclipsed by Oklahoma with 768 yards against Kansas State in 1988.

386. The "Scoring Explosion" blasted the opposition for a phenomenal 84 touchdowns in 12 games.

Mike Rozier

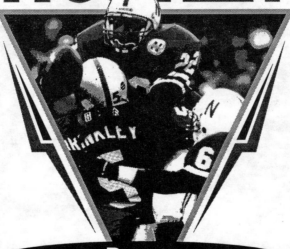

7

HUSKER TRIVIA

DEFENSE

387. Tom Osborne's teams have been noted more for their offensive might than their defensive prowess. However, one of his teams tallied three consecutive shutouts. In what season did this take place and who were the victims?

388. What were the most pass interceptions made by a Nebraska defense in one game?

389. Name the N.U. defender who had the most blocked punts for touchdowns in a season. How many?

390. In Charlie McBride's 12 years as Nebraska defensive coordinator, 1982-93, how many times have the Huskers ranked in the top 15 nationally in total defense?

391. Linebacker Lee Kunz who lettered 1976-78 also excelled in another sport for Nebraska. What was his other specialty?

392. What was the longest scoring run by a defensive lineman at Nebraska? Who made the run?

393. What is the greatest number of points allowed by an N.U. defense in a season?

394. Who established Nebraska's single season mark for quarterback sacks?

395. Which Husker defender had the most interception returns for touchdowns in his career? How many?

387. Nebraska crushed three consecutive opponents in 1979. The Huskers shut out New Mexico State 57-0, Kansas 42-0 and Oklahoma State 36-0 for a combined score of 135-0 for three games.

388. During the Kansas State game in 1970 the Huskers had sticky fingers indeed. That day they picked off 7 Wildcat passes enroute to a 51-13 N.U. victory.

389. Wayne Meylan proved to be the right man in the right place at the right time in 1966 when he was able to score two touchdowns after blocking punts.

390. Though he has sometimes been maligned by Husker fans, McBride can point with pride to the fact that his players have ranked in the top 15 in total defense 10 of those 13 years.

391. Kunz was also a successful competitor in track and field. He won the Big Eight discus championship in 1978.

392. Leroy Zentic ran the ball 36 yards for a touchdown in the great 1959 upset win over Oklahoma. He came up with a muffed Sooner quick kick and returned it for a score. The loss was the first in the conference for Oklahoma in 75 outings. They had not been beaten since 1946 when Kansas was victorious 16-13.

393. The 1948 team possesses the dubious distinction of having allowed 10 opponents to score a remarkable 273 points in a futile 2-8-0 season.

394. Trev Alberts set the mark of 15 quarterback sacks in his Butkus Award winning season of 1993.

395. Dave Mason managed to score 3 touchdowns on 8 interceptions during his Husker career, 1969-71.

396. The venerable Pop Warner was quoted as calling one N.U. defender "the greatest tackle who ever lived." Of whom was Warner speaking?

397. Name the Husker defender who set the school record for the most total tackles made in his career.

398. Which former All-American Husker defensive tackle became only the second deaf player to successfully compete in the NFL?

399. Which N.U. player had the most blocked kicks in a season for the Huskers?

400. What is the greatest number of shutouts recorded by an N.U. defense in one season?

401. What were the fewest number of points allowed in a season by a Nebraska defense since the sport has been played at the school?

402. What is the greatest number of points that Nebraska has surrendered to an opponent in one quarter?

403. The great N.U. linebacker, Steve Damkroger, had a brother who played on the illustrious 1971 championship team. Who was he and what position did he play?

404. The longest touchdown run against the Huskers was made by an amazing athlete who almost attended Nebraska. Who was this superstar and how long was the run?

405. Name the Husker defender who had the most interception yards in his career.

396. Warner was complimenting none other than Ed Weir, Nebraska All-American 1924-25, and one of the greatest competitors to ever don a Husker uniform.

397. Tough Jerry Murtaugh gave opposing teams fits during his career at N.U., 1968-70, as he made an incredible 339 total tackles.

398. Kenny Walker, always a crowd favorite, had a brief but successful stint with the Denver Broncos. He was an inspiration to the fans in Denver.

399. Barron Miles blocked four kicks in 1994 to set the school record.

400. The Huskers had a remarkable string of 10 straight shutouts in 1902 to establish a school record that will probably never be broken.

401. Twice Nebraska has shut out all of the opponents faced in a season—in 1890 during a two game season and in 1902 during a ten game season.

402. Nebraska was totally shellshocked at UCLA in 1988. By the time the dust had settled in the first quarter, the Huskers were down by 28-0. They went on to lose the game 41-28.

403. His name was Maury and he played fullback for the Huskers (lettered 1971-73).

404. Gale Sayers, a Kansas University back from Omaha, broke loose and galloped for a 99 yard touchdown run against the Huskers in a 23-9 Nebraska victory in 1963.

405. Bill Kosch returned 10 interceptions for 233 yards during his Husker career (lettered 1969-71).

406. In which year did the Huskers have the greatest turnover margin?

407. What is the lowest rushing total given up in a game by an N.U. defense and who was the opponent?

408. In modern times (since 1950), what is the fewest number of passes that the Husker defense has been able to intercept in one season?

409. Which Nebraska defensive player had the most unassisted tackles in a season?

410. Nebraska has led the nation in total defense twice since World War II. In what years did this happen?

411. Which N.U. player made the most fumble recoveries in one season?

412. What is the record for the lowest total defensive average maintained by an N.U. team in modern times (since 1950) over the course of an entire season?

413. What were the most interceptions made by an N.U. defense in a season?

414. What major injury sidelined No.1 free safety Mike Minter for the remainder of the 1994 season?

406. The great 1971 team, perhaps the finest in history, recorded a remarkable turnover margin of +26 with 47 total takeaways. No other team has had a margin higher than +18.

407. When the Huskers played Kansas State in 1976 they were very stingy indeed. The Wildcats only managed a minus 45 yards rushing that day against Nebraska.

408. The Huskers only managed to pick off 6 passes in 1958 and 1961 to establish this dubious record of achievement. Since the record in 1958 was 3-7-0 and in 1961 it was 3-6-1, their defensive performance was reflected on the scoreboard.

409. Jerry Murtaugh had an incredible 71 unassisted tackles in 1970, Nebraska's first national championship year.

410. The Huskers were first in 1967 with 157.6 yards per game allowed and in 1984 with 203.3 yards per game allowed.

411. Broderick Thomas recovered an amazing six fumbles in 1986 to set the school record.

412. The record for modern times is the impressive 157.6 yard average per game allowed by N.U. in the 10 game season of 1967.

413. The Huskers stopped many a drive by their opponents in 1970. During that season Nebraska picked off 30 passes in their first national championship year.

414. Minter, the quarterback of the Husker defense early in the 1994 campaign, blew out a knee in the third quarter of the Texas Tech game, the second game of the season.

415. Name the player who had the most total tackles at Nebraska in a single season.

416. What are the fewest passing yards given up by an N.U. defense in a season?

417. Which Nebraska defender made the most pass interceptions in one season?

418. Which Husker player holds the school record for passes broken up in a season?

419. What were the fewest touchdowns allowed by a modern (since 1950) Nebraska defense in a season?

420. Which Nebraska defender fell on the Billy Sims fumble at the end of the 1978 Oklahoma game that preserved the Huskers' 17-14 victory?

421. In what season did Nebraska lead the nation in scoring defense?

422. Which N.U. player had the most interceptions for touchdowns in a season?

423. What are the fewest yards rushing given up in a season by Nebraska?

424. Which player had the most assisted tackles in his career at Nebraska?

415. Lee Kunz set the tackle mark for a single season by registering a total of 141 tackles in 1977.

416. The Huskers gave up a paltry 439 yards passing in 11 games in 1973, Tom Osborne's first season as head coach.

417. Three Huskers lead the way with 7 interceptions during a season at Nebraska. Larry Wachholtz picked off 7 in 1966, Dana Stephenson matched that total in 1969 and Bill Kosch intercepted 7 in 1970.

418. The great Husker defensive back, Barron Miles, set the record of 13 passes broken up during the 1994 season.

419. The mark for the fewest TDs allowed by a Husker defense was set in 1981 when a measly 9 scores were made by N.U. opponents in a 9-2-0 regular season.

420. Jim Pillen fell on the loose ball at the N.U. 3 yard line. It was probably the biggest play of his Husker career.

421. Ironically, the Huskers led the nation with 9.5 points per game in 1984 after leading the nation in scoring offense with 52.0 points in 1983. Imagine if they could have put the two halves together in the same season.

422. Dave Mason was able to score 3 touchdowns on 6 interceptions in the national championship year of 1971.

423. In 1967 the Huskers gave up only 675 yards rushing in the entire season. That is an average of only 67.5 yards a game.

424. The incomparable Jerry Murtaugh recorded 191 assisted tackles during his great N.U. career (lettered 1968-70).

425. In 1993 the Huskers were the victims of the most passing yards ever by a Big Eight quarterback in a single game. Who was the quarterback and for whom did he play?

426. What is the lowest rushing average allowed by N.U. 's defense in a season?

427. Name the N.U. defenders who have intercepted the most passes in one game. How many passes did they intercept?

428. Which player had the most assisted tackles in a season at Nebraska?

429. Who is Nebraska's career quarterback sack leader?

430. What is the lowest per game passing average allowed by an N.U. defense in a season?

431. Name the Husker defender who had the longest interception return that did not result in a touchdown. How long was it?

432. Name the Husker player who had the longest interception for a touchdown. How long was the return?

433. Name the Nebraska defensive player who had the most unassisted tackles in his career.

434. Which Husker defender made the most pass interceptions in his career? How many?

435. Nebraska has led the nation in pass defense twice since World War II. During which seasons did this take place?

425. Chad May of Kansas State bombed the Husker secondary for an incredible 489 yards on October 16, 1993. Fortunately Nebraska had enough offense to outscore the Wildcats, 45-28.

426. In 1967 the Huskers allowed 10 opponents 67.5 yards rushing per game.

427. Three players have each intercepted 3 passes in one game. They are Dana Stephenson against Colorado in 1969, Joe Blahak against Kansas State in 1970 and Ric Lindquist against Kansas State in 1979.

428. Lee Kunz had 95 tackle assists in 1977 to set the school record.

429. Butkus Award winner, Trev Alberts, established the career mark with 29 1/2 sacks, 1990-93.

430. The Huskers allowed a paltry 39.9 yards per game passing in 1973 to establish the school mark.

431. Bret Clark returned an interception 68 yards against Minnesota on September 15, 1984 and was tackled before he could reach the goal line.

432. Willie Greenfield returned an interception 95 yards for a touchdown against Colorado in 1955. Bill Kosch matched that feat against Texas A&M in 1971.

433. The great Steve Damkroger had 157 unassisted tackles in his long and productive career at Nebraska, 1979-82.

434. Dana Stephenson intercepted 14 passes in his career at Nebraska (lettered 1967-69).

435. The Huskers led the nation in 1973 with a 39.9 yards per game average and in 1981 with a 100.1 yards per game average.

Trev Alberts

8

HUSKER TRIVIA

NICKNAMES

436. Who had the nickname "Thunder" at Nebraska?

437. Who had the nickname "The Turmanator" on the Husker squad in 1994?

438. What is the top defensive unit at Nebraska called and why are they known by that nickname?

439. Who had the nickname "Zippety" on the Husker team?

440. Who was fondly known as "Twinkle Toes" by the Husker team?

441. Which N.U. player was also known by the nickname "Big Fig?"

442. Who at Nebraska went by the nickname of "Doc?"

443. Who were known as the "We Backs" at Nebraska?

444. Name the Nebraska player who went by the nickname "Big Ed" during his football career.

436. He was none other than Bill "Thunder" Thornton, Bob Devaney's first great Husker back, who lettered 1960-62.

437. Matt Turman, walk-on quarterback who started the Kansas State game for the injured Brook Berringer, earned this colorful nickname.

438. The top defensive unit is called the Blackshirts because they wear black jerseys in practice to distinguish them from the lower defensive units.

439. Fred "Zippety" Duda will long be fondly remembered as one of Nebraska's most gutsy quarterbacks. He lettered for the Huskers 1963-65.

440. Jim "Twinkle Toes" Baffico lettered for Bob Devaney's first Husker team in 1962. As you might have guessed from his nickname, he was not exactly a lightweight.

441. Bob "Big Fig" Newton lettered at Nebraska 1969-70. He was named All-American at tackle in 1970. Newton had a long NFL career, 1971-80, with Chicago and Seattle.

442. E.J. "Doc" Stewart was the head coach of the Nebraska Cornhuskers, 1916-17. His team won two Missouri Valley championships.

443. Derek Brown and Calvin Jones earned this nickname for the way that they worked as a running back tandem in 1992.

444. One of the Husker's all-time great players, "Big Ed" Weir lettered at N.U. 1923-25 and went on to a brief but successful pro career with the Frankfort Yellowjackets, 1926-28.

445. Who at Nebraska had the nickname "Indian?"

446. Who at Nebraska went by the nickname of "Bummy?"

447. Who at Nebraska was known by the nickname "Jumbo?"

448. Name the player who was called the "Wild Hoss" when he was making his mark as a Husker.

449. Name the person at Nebraska who went by the nickname "Potsy?"

450. Who had the nickname "Train Wreck" during his N.U. career?

451. Which team was nicknamed the "Scoring Explosion?"

452. Who do you think was known as "Breakaway Bobby" during his Husker playing days? Throw away your letter sweater if you can't guess this one!

453. Who as Nebraska was better known as "Biff?"

445. Henry Frank "Indian" Schulte was the head coach of the Huskers 1919-20. He also went by the nickname "Pa."

446. Walter C. "Bummy" Booth was the head coach at Nebraska 1900-05. His great 1902 team went 10-0-0 and was not only undefeated but also unscored upon. At one point during Booth's tenure, his teams won 27 straight games.

447. E.O. "Jumbo" Stiehm was a very successful head coach at Nebraska. During his tenure as coach 1911-15, his team went 29 games without a defeat.

448. Lloyd "Wild Hoss" Cardwell lettered at Nebraska 1934-36 and was drafted in the first round as a halfback by the Detroit Lions. He went on to play with the Lions for 7 years, 1937-43.

449. George "Potsy" Clark was the Husker head coach twice, in 1945 and then again in 1948.

450. Tom "Train Wreck" Novak, Husker All-American, was a man who played his heart out on every down on teams whose records were dismal. He was one of the few bright lights to shine for the Huskers after the Rose Bowl year.

451. The awesome 1983 Husker team earned the nickname for the imaginative and frequent ways they found to put points on the board.

452. Yes, of course, "Breakaway Bobby" was the great Bobby Reynolds who gave Husker fans the greatest single season of thrills ever by a back until Mike Rozier matched him in 1983.

453. L. Mc C. Jones, the head coach who led the Huskers to the 1941 Rose Bowl, went by the more easily remembered nickname of "Biff." He was the N.U. head coach from 1937 to 1941.

454. Who had the nickname "Lighthorse" during his Husker playing days?

455. Name the player who had the nickname "Marvelous" during his Husker career.

456. Which Nebraska player had the nickname "The Leg" during his Husker years?

457. Who at Nebraska had the nickname "Mad Dog?"

458. Who was called "Dollar Bill" at Nebraska?

459. Who was fond of calling Memorial Stadium "Our House" and proclaiming that he had the key?

460. Which Nebraska player went by the initials "I.M.?"

461. Name the player who had the nickname "Choo-Choo" during his days as a Husker.

462. Who at Nebraska is called the "Fat Fox?"

454. "Lighthorse" was alternately known as Harry Wilson, one of Bob Devaney's great early running backs. He lettered at Nebraska 1964-66.

455. "Marvelous" Jarvis Redwine truly did live up to his nickname during his Husker days. This great I-back broke some fantastic long runs during his N.U. career (lettered 1979-80).

456. Craig Johnson, the reserve I-back who always had big days against Kansas, was known as "The Leg." Johnson lettered at N.U. 1978-80.

457. The player with this colorful nickname was none other than Jack Hazen who lettered at Nebraska 1941-42, 1946 and 1948.

458. "Dollar Bill" Bryant, who lettered at Nebraska in 1978, gained this distinctive nickname because of his habit of keeping at least one dollar bill in his pocket at all times so he would never be completely broke.

459. Broderick Thomas, Nebraska's All-American outside linebacker during the late 1980s wasn't shy about promoting this name. Most of the time Broderick and his team members could back up the challenge.

460. "I.M." stood for Isaiah Moses in I.M. Hipp's name. He provided Huskers fans with many thrills during his I-back days at N.U., 1977-79.

461. "Choo-Choo" Charlie Winters, the fine Husker running back, really did resemble a runaway freight train once he got his legs churning. He lettered at Nebraska, 1965-66.

462. He is none other than Don Bryant, N.U. Associate Athletic Director and Community Relations Director.

463. Name the Husker player who was also known as the "Tecumseh Tornado" during his playing days.

464. Which great Nebraska player was given the nickname "The Dealer" during his N.U. career?

465. Name the player who had the nickname "The Dodger" at Nebraska.

466. Name the player who was known by the nickname "Slick."

467. Who had the nickname "No Pain" at Nebraska?

468. Which Husker player had the nickname "The Mosquito" during his football career?

469. Who had the nickname "The Jet" at Nebraska?

470. Whom did the press refer to as "Michael Heisman" at Nebraska?

463. Tony Davis, the great I-back/fullback, truly was a tornado on the football field and surely made the town of Tecumseh very proud by his gridiron exploits during his playing career (lettered 1973-75).

464. Dave "The Dealer" Humm, from Las Vegas, dealt the Huskers many a winning had as quarterback at Nebraska (lettered 1972-74).

465. Roger Craig, the great I-back/fullback, earned this nickname for his great elusive moves as a runner during his Husker career (lettered 1980-82).

466. Anthony Steels indeed was a slick wingback for Nebraska. He had some incredible pass receptions and runs for the Huskers (lettered 1979-81).

467. Wayne Meylan earned this moniker because of the way he sent ball carriers to dream land with a minimum of fuss. He created terror in many an opponent's backfield during his career as a Husker, 1965-67.

468. Chuck Malito was called "The Mosquito" because he was so thin. Make no mistake, though, he had a lot of toughness packed inside his slender body. He made some unbelievable catches for the Huskers during his Husker career (lettered 1974-76).

469. "The Jet" was none other than the fleet-footed Johnny Rodgers who won the Heisman Trophy in 1972.

470. Mike Rozier was given that nickname during the 1983 season and indeed it proved to be prophetic as he was awarded the coveted Heisman Trophy at the end of the season.

471. Name the Nebraska player who had the nickname "The Flyer" during his Husker career.

472. Who was known as "Tough Tony" during his Husker playing days?

473. Which group of players on the 1994 national championship team had the nickname "The Pipeline?"

474. Name four of the colorful nicknames that had variously been applied to the Nebraska football team before the name "Cornhuskers" finally stuck.

475. Which Husker had the nickname "Sandman" at Nebraska?

476. Who was alternately known as "J.R. Superstar" at Nebraska?

477. Name the player who was nicknamed "The Fly" during his Husker football days.

478. Which Nebraska player had the nickname "Link" during his football career?

471. He was none other than Irving "The Flyer" Fryar who lettered at N.U. 1981-83. Irving was Nebraska's greatest wingback since the superb Johnny Rodgers.

472. "Tough Tony" Davis, Husker I-back/fullback, gave the fans a lot to cheer about during his playing career at Nebraska (lettered 1973-75). He always gave the fans and the coaches 110% effort whenever he stepped on the field.

473. This illustrious group was the offensive line of Rob Zatechka, Joel Wilks, Aaron Graham and Brendan Stai. Many observers rated them as the best Nebraska offensive line in school history.

474. The team at one time or another prior to 1900 had been called "Bug-Eaters," "Rattlesnake Boys," "Antelopes" and "Old Gold Knights."

475. All-American Broderick Thomas liked this nickname because as an awesome outside linebacker he liked to put opposing ball-carriers to sleep with powerful hits.

476. Surely you remember that Johnny Rodgers had this nickname and he lived up to it every time he stepped onto the playing field.

477. Guy "The Fly" Ingles, N.U. split end, was given this nickname because of his diminutive size. No one ever doubted the size of his heart and the amount of courage he displayed during his Husker career (lettered 1968-70).

478. William R. "Link" Lyman was a star tackle for N.U. in the early '20s. He played 11 seasons of pro football and is in the Pro Football Hall of Fame.

479. Name the player who had the colorful nickname of "Big Moose" during his Husker years.

480. Who was the player who was known by the nickname of "Wild Bill?"

481. How did coach "Jumbo" Stiehm get his nickname?

482. Who had the nickname of "Jug" during his Husker playing career?

483. Name the player who went by the nickname "Choppy" during his Husker playing days.

484. Which Husker player had the nickname "Hippity" during his N.U. career?

485. Who at Nebraska was nicknamed "The Senator?"

486. Which N.U. player was also known as the "Shenendoah Kid" while he performed on the gridiron?

479. Dave "The Big Moose" Noble was a standout player from Omaha Central High who lettered 1921-23. He was twice named all-conference as a running back.

480. "Wild Bill" Callahan was a fine running back who lettered for the Huskers 1936-38 and played for the Detroit Lions 1940-45. He was a large back, for the era he played in, tipping the scales at 200 pounds and standing 6-feet, 3-inches tall.

481. As you might guess, it resulted from his size. He was a "big" center on Wisconsin's football team and a member of the Badger's basketball team.

482. John "Jug" Brown lettered at Nebraska 1925-27. He was a genuine triple threat back who captained the 1927 Husker squad.

483. John "Choppy" Rhodes lettered at Nebraska 1923-25. He played end, fullback and halfback for the Huskers and was All-Missouri Valley in 1924 and 1925. Rhodes was later the Nebraska baseball coach and Wyoming athletic director.

484. He was none other than the great Harry "Hippity" Hopp who lettered at Nebraska 1938-40. Hopp was twice named All-Big Six back 1939-40. He later played with the Detroit Lions of the NFL. "Hippity" was a member of the illustrious Rose Bowl team of 1940.

485. Ray "The Senator" Prochaska lettered at Nebraska 1938-40. He was named an All-Big Six end in 1940 and played on the 1940 Rose Bowl team. He played one year of pro ball with the Cleveland Rams in 1941.

486. He was otherwise known as Van Brownson, who alternated at quarterback with Jerry Tagge, 1969-71.

487. When was the nickname "Cornhusker" first applied to the Nebraska team and who came up with the name?

488. What did the D.X. stand for in head coach D.X. Bible's name?

489. What is a "bugeater", the inspiration for one of Nebraska's early team nicknames?

490. Who was nicknamed the "Cambridge Crusher" at Nebraska?

491. Who was called "The Prince" during his Husker playing days?

492. One of Jumbo Stiehm"s guards on the great 1915 team was nicknamed "Mother", believe it or not. Who was this player?

493. Who was fondly known as "Champ" at Nebraska?

494. What was "Vike" Francis' real first name?

495. John "Choppy" Rhodes had a relative who played at Nebraska and had a distinctive nickname as you might guess. What was it?

487. In 1900, it was Cy Sherman, a Lincoln Star sports writer, who applied this moniker to the Nebraska team. It was much better than the previous nicknames that the team had been known by and it stuck.

488. The initials stood for Dana Xenophon, which makes it clear why he went by his initials.

489. A bugeater is actually an insect-eating bull bat that is commonly found on the prairie. It is still a very strange nickname.

490. The "Crusher" was none other than All-American tackle Jerry Minnick who lettered 1951-53.

491. He was none other than Vince "The Prince" Ferragamo, All-American quarterback for the Huskers and L.A. Rams signal-caller.

492. His real name was Earle Abbott, a 210-pound All-Missouri Valley player from David City, Nebraska. It was wise to smile when you called him "Mother."

493. Guy "Champ" Chamberlin was an All-American end in 1915 and he was probably Nebraska's best known player from the early days. In the hearts of Husker fans Chamberlin truly was a champ.

494. Fullback Francis had the interesting name of Viscount, which probably explains why he went by the nickname. He starred in the 1941 Rose Bowl game against Stanford.

495. Roscoe Rhodes was a Husker tackle in the late teens and was known as "Dusty" Rhodes. He lettered at Nebraska 1916-17.

496. What was the popular term for the Nebraska team when Jumbo Stiehm was the head coach?

497. Who was known as "Earth, Wind and Fryar?"

496. The were fondly known as the "Stiehm-Rollers" after the fashion in which they crushed their opponents.

497. Sportswriters liked to call Turner Gill, Mike Rozier and Irving Fryar by this name. The nickname spoke of the scoring power of this trio.

I.M. Hipp

9

TRIVIA

AWARDS AND HONORS

498. Which Nebraska great was named to the nation's All-American Centennial Team?

499. How many NFL first round draft picks has Nebraska had?

500. Which major award did All-American Trev Alberts win in his senior year of 1993?

501. U.P.I.'s Big Eight Player of the Year in 1966 wasn't just another pretty face. Who was he?

502. Who was Nebraska's first Lombardi Trophy winner?

503. How many two-time All-Americans has Nebraska had during Tom Osborne's coaching tenure?

504. How many academic All-Americans has Nebraska had?

505. Who was Nebraska's first All-American ball-carrier?

506. How many draft picks has Nebraska averaged each year since 1954?

507. Who was named the Most Valuable Player of the "Game of the Century" in 1971?

498. The immortal Ed Weir was named as tackle in 1969 along with such greats as Red Grange, Bronco Nagurski and Tom Harmon.

499. N.U. has had 26 first round draft picks through 1994--3 in 1937, 2 in 1964, 3 in 1972, 1 in 1973, 1 in 1974, 1 in 1975, 2 in 1979, 1 in 1980, 1 in 1982, 1 in 1983, 3 in 1984, 1 in 1987, 1 in 1988, 1 in 1989, 2 in 1991, 1 in 1992 and 1 in 1994.

500. Trev brought home the Butkus Award in 1993. The trophy honors the nation's top linebacker each year.

501. Old Number 66, Wayne "No Pain" Meylan, Nebraska's middle guard, was everybody's All-American in 1966. Meylan played with tremendous intensity and struck fear in the hearts of opposing ball carriers.

502. Rich Glover won the coveted prize, along with the Outland Trophy, in 1972.

503. The Huskers have had 5 repeat winners. They are Rik Bonness, 1974-75, Dave Rimington, 1981-82, Mike Rozier, 1982-83, Broderick Thomas, 1987-88 and Jake Young, 1988-89.

504. The Huskers have had 52 academic All-Americans from 1960 to 1994, including four in 1982.

505. Guy Chamberlin was named All-American end in 1915.

506. Year in and year out the Huskers have averaged over five draft picks a year for the past 40 years.

507. Jerry Tagge was so honored in the 35-31 Husker victory. Tagge rushed for 49 yards on 17 carries and completed 6 of 12 passes for 65 yards.

508. The Huskers had three players selected in the first round of the NFL draft in 1937. Who were they?

509. Nebraska has had three quarterbacks named Academic All-Americans. Name them.

510. Nebraska players have won the prestigious Lombardi Trophy three times. Which players have won this award and when?

511. Whose number was the first to be retired by Nebraska?

512. Who was named the college defensive player of the year by Football News in 1993?

513. Who was Nebraska's first All-American under the leadership of Bob Devaney?

514. Tom Novak was named all-conference at 4 different positions. Name them.

515. Which Nebraska lineman is the only college player to win the Outland Trophy two years in a row?

516. Who was the last N.U. All-American in the pre-Devaney era?

517. Which Nebraska players were named Big Eight Offensive Players of the Year in 1992?

508. Lloyd Cardwell was selected as a halfback by the Detroit Lions. Sam Francis was chosen as a halfback by the Philadelphia Eagles. Les McDonald was selected as an end by the Chicago Bears.

509. Dennis Claridge made the team in 1963, Vince Ferragamo was named in 1976 and Gerry Gdowski was named to the team in 1989.

510. Rich Glover won the Lombardi in 1972, Dave Rimington won in 1982 and Dean Steinkuhler was awarded the Lombardi in 1983.

511. No. 60, that was worn by Tom "Train Wreck" Novak, was the first number to be retired by the Huskers.

512. Butkus Award winner Trev Alberts was honored by Football News as the premier defensive player of 1993.

513. Bob Brown was named All-American as a guard in 1963.

514. Tom "Train Wreck" Novak was honored as a fullback in 1946, center and guard in 1947, center and linebacker in 1948 and 1949.

515. Dave Rimington, the premier Husker center, won the award in 1981 and 1982.

516. Jerry Minnick was named All-American as a tackle in 1952. The Huskers did not have another player so honored until Bob Brown in 1963.

517. Calvin Jones was named as Player of the Year by the Big Eight coaches. His running mate, Derek Brown, was proclaimed Player of the Year by the Associated Press.

518. Which Husker player was named Big Eight Freshman of the Year in 1992?

519. Nebraska had two All-American ends in 1965. Who were they?

520. Nebraska players have won the Outland Trophy six times. Which players have won this award?

521. Who was Nebraska's last three-time all-conference player?

522. In 1964 the Huskers had two players chosen in the first round of the NFL draft. Who were they?

523. How many Husker jerseys have been retired and to whom did the jerseys belong?

524. Which Husker player was named Big Eight Defensive Freshman of the Year in 1990 by conference coaches?

525. Who was the only Nebraska player to be named all-conference for four straight years?

526. Who was Nebraska's first All-Big Eight player?

527. Which rookie professional player from Nebraska was named All-Pro in 1993 as a return specialist?

518. Tommie Frazier made an immediate impact on the league and was given this honor by Big Eight coaches.

519. Both Tony Jeter and Freeman White were honored as All-Americans in 1965. They provided many thrills for Husker fans during their playing careers.

520. Larry Jacobson won it in 1971, Rich Glover won in 1972, Dave Rimington won it in 1981 and 1982, Dean Steinkuhler won in 1983, Will Shields won in 1992 and, finally, Zach Wiegert won the Outland in 1994.

521. Standout All-American right tackle Zach Wiegert was named All-Big Eight in 1992, 1993 and 1994.

522. Bob Brown was selected as a guard by the Philadelphia Eagles. Lloyd Voss was chosen as a tackle by the Green Bay Packers.

523. By the end of the 1993 season, six numbers have been retired. The are #60 of Tom Novak, #20 of Johnny Rodgers, #79 of Rich Glover, #50 of Dave Rimington, #71 of Dean Steinkuhler and #30 of Mike Rozier.

524. Future All-American and Butkus Award winner, Trev Alberts, was recognized early by coaches for his obvious potential.

525. Tom Novak has this distinction. He was honored each year, 1946-49.

526. Don Olson, a guard, was so honored in 1959.

527. Tyrone Hughes showed enough of his punt and kickoff return brilliance to be named to this elite group. He made his mark with the New Orleans Saints.

528. How many All-American centers has Tom Osborne had at Nebraska since he took over as head coach in 1973?

529. In 1972 the Huskers had three players chosen in the first round of the NFL draft. Who were they?

530. Which Nebraska player was awarded the school's sixth Outland Trophy in 1992.

531. In the 1970 season, which Nebraska player was named Big Eight Player of the Year?

532. Nebraska has twice had the Outland, Lombardi and Heisman Trophies awarded in the same year. When did this happen and who won the awards?

533. Who were the four co-captains of the "Scoring Explosion" team in 1983?

534. In 1973 the Huskers had one player chosen in the first round of the NFL draft. Who was he?

535. Who was the first recipient of the Guy Chamberlin Trophy at Nebraska?

536. Who was the second Nebraska tight end to be selected in the first round of the NFL draft?

528. Osborne has coached six All-American centers during his tenure as head coach at Nebraska—Rik Bonness in 1974-75, Tom Davis in 1977, Dave Rimington in 1981-82, Mark Traynowicz in 1984, Bill Lewis in 1985 and Jake Young in 1988-89.

529. Jeff Kinney was selected as a halfback by the Kansas City Chiefs. Larry Jacobson was chosen as a tackle by the New York Giants. Jerry Tagge was selected as a quarterback by the Green Bay Packers.

530. Offensive guard Will Shields, a consensus All-American and future Kansas City Chief, received the prestigious Outland Trophy in 1992.

531. Jerry Murtaugh, Nebraska's All-American linebacker (and co-captain), was chosen for this honor. He beat out Lynn Dickey, the great Kansas State quarterback, for the award.

532. In 1972 Rich Glover won the Outland and Lombardi Trophies while Johnny Rodgers won the Heisman. In 1983 Dean Steinkuhler won both the Outland and Lombardi Trophies while Mike Rozier won the Heisman Trophy.

533. The co-captains were Turner Gill, Mike Keeler, Dean Steinkuhler and Mike Tranmer.

534. Johnny Rodgers was selected as a halfback by the San Diego Chargers.

535. The first recipient of the award, in 1967, was Marv Mueller, a 192 pound safety.

536. Johnny Mitchell was chosen in the first round of the 1992 pro draft by the New York Jets. The first tight end taken in the first round was Junior Miller in 1980 by the Atlanta Falcons.

537. Tom Osborne, as a football player, was the first individual to win two certain Omaha World-Herald awards. What are these two honors?

538. Who was the Husker player selected in the first round of the NFL draft in 1974?

539. Who was Nebraska's seventh Outland Trophy winner?

540. Which N.U. team has been voted by many experts as the best college team of all time?

541. How many defensive ends have been named All-America at Nebraska since 1971?

542. Name the only Nebraska Cornhusker member of the National Football Foundation Hall of Fame who is also a member of the Pro Football Hall of Fame.

543. How many All-American quarterbacks has Nebraska had in the Devaney-Osborne era? Who were they?

544. How many All-American tight ends has Tom Osborne had at Nebraska since 1973?

537. Osborne was the World-Herald's Nebraska High School Athlete of the Year in 1954 and also the World-Herald College Athlete of the Year in 1958.

538. John Dutton was chosen as a tackle by the Baltimore Colts.

539. Zach Wiegert, Nebraska's standout right tackle, claimed the coveted award in the Husker's 1994 national championship season.

540. The inimitable national championship team of 1971 has often been called the greatest of all time.

541. N.U. has had 8 All-American defensive ends since 1971. Willie Harper was named in 1971-72, Bob Martin in 1975, George Andrews in 1978, Derrie Nelson in 1980 and Jimmy Williams in 1981. As outside linebackers Broderick Thomas was named All-American in 1987-88, Travis Hill in 1992 and Trev Alberts in 1993.

542. The great Guy Chamberlin was inducted into the National Football Foundation Hall of Fame in 1962 and into the Pro Football Hall of Fame in 1965.

543. Nebraska has had four All-American quarterbacks since 1962—Jerry Tagge in 1971, Dave Humm in 1974, Vince Ferragamo in 1976 and Steve Taylor in 1987.

544. Osborne has coached only one All-American tight end during his tenure at Nebraska. He was none other than Junior Miller in 1979.

545. Whom was the last Husker named to the College Football Hall of Fame?

546. Who was Nebraska's first participant in the Hula Bowl?

547. An N.U. back was the first player west of the Mississippi to be named to the Walter Camp All-American team. Who was he?

548. During which pro draft did Nebraska have the most players chosen?

549. Who were Nebraska's two first round NFL draft choices in 1979?

550. Who is Nebraska's only sophomore to be named an All-American?

551. Who was the last Husker named a team captain two years in a row?

552. Which Husker player was selected in the first round of the NFL draft in 1980?

553. Nebraska had three first round draft picks in the 1984 pro draft. Who were they?

554. When Mike Rozier won the Heisman Trophy in 1983, did N.U. have any other major vote-getter in the balloting?

545. Rich Glover, an All-American nose guard in 1971 and 1972 and winner of the Outland Trophy and Lombardi Award in 1972, was inducted in 1995. He joined 12 others inducted in that year, including Jim Brown and Billy Sims.

546. He was Kent McCloughan, Nebraska fullback, who played in the 1965 Hula Bowl game.

547. R.E. Benedict was named to a halfback spot on Camp's third team in 1898.

548. In 1975 the Huskers had 12 players taken in the pro draft, including Tom Ruud by Buffalo in the first round.

549. George Andrews was selected as a linebacker by the Los Angeles Rams. Kelvin Clark was chosen as a tackle by the Denver Broncos.

550. The great Bobby Reynolds was the only player so named after his banner 1950 season.

551. Not since 1950 and 1951, when Robert Mullen was named both years, has a player been a team captain during more than one season at Nebraska.

552. Junior Miller was chosen as a tight end by the Atlanta Falcons.

553. Those chosen in the first round were Irving Fryar by the New England Patriots, Dean Steinkuhler by the Houston Oilers and Mike Rozier by the Houston Oilers.

554. Yes, Turner Gill was 4th with 190 points. Rozier had 1801 points, Steve Young of BYU had 1172 points and Doug Flutie of Boston College had 253 points.

555. Elmer Dohrmann, an all-conference end for N.U., has the distinction of winning the most sports letters in his career. How many letters did Elmer win?

556. Which Husker was chosen in the first round of the 1988 pro draft?

557. Who was the first recipient of the Tom Novak Award at Nebraska?

558. For which award was Ed Stewart a finalist in 1994?

559. Nebraska had two players chosen in the first round of the 1991 pro draft. Name them.

560. Who were the first N.U. players to participate in the Senior Bowl?

561. Name the first members inducted into the Nebraska Football Hall of Fame.

562. Which Husker was selected in the first round of the 1989 pro draft?

563. Nebraska has 5 ex-coaches in the National Football Hall of Fame. Name them.

564. Who was N.U.'s first black player to be named season co-captain of a Husker football team?

555. Dohrmann won an incredible 11 letters, 3 in football, 3 in baseball, 3 in basketball and 2 in track.

556. Neil Smith, the great Nebraska defensive player, was selected by the Kansas City Chiefs in 1988. He later became an All-Pro for the Chiefs.

557. The first recipient of the award was tackle Charles Toogood who won the honor in 1950.

558. All-American linebacker Stewart almost gave Nebraska back-to-back winners of the Lombardi Trophy with Trev Alberts. He finished behind the eventual winner, Dana Howard of Illinois.

559. Bruce Pickens, Husker defensive back, was chosen in the first round by the Atlanta Falcons. In addition, Mike Croel, Nebraska outside linebacker, was picked by the Denver Broncos.

560. Joe Bordogna, Nebraska quarterback, and Jerry Minnick, N.U. tackle, participated in the Senior Bowl of 1953.

561. Ed Weir, Guy Chamberlin and George Sauer were all elected in 1971 to the Hall of Fame.

562. The incomparable outside linebacker and character, Broderick Thomas, was picked in the first round by the Tampa Bay Buccaneers.

563. They are Fielding Yost, D.X. Bible, Biff Jones, E.N. Robinson and Bob Devaney.

564. Bill "Thunder" Thornton was the first black player to be so honored. Others had been single game captains but Thornton was the first to be honored for an entire season.

565. Name the Husker player who was selected in the first round of the 1992 pro football draft.

566. Which Husker player was selected in the first round of the NFL draft in 1982?

567. Who was named the UPI Lineman of the Year in 1994?

568. Which player was named the Big Eight Defensive Player of the Year in 1993?

569. Who was Nebraska's first black All-American?

570. Who were Nebraska's two All-American middle guards during Bob Devaney's coaching years?

571. Which 1975 Husker Academic All-American later became a Nebraska team physician?

572. Who was the first Nebraska running back to be named All-Big Eight and when was he so honored?

573. Which Husker player was selected in the first round of the NFL draft in 1983?

574. What was the purpose of the "Double Hundred" celebration?

565. Johnny Mitchell, Nebraska's tight end who was the first Husker player to leave school early to enter the pro draft, was picked in the first round of the 1992 draft by the New York Jets.

566. Jimmy Williams was chosen as a linebacker by the Detroit Lions.

567. Outland Trophy winner and All-American Zach Wigert was given this honor after Nebraska's national championship season.

568. All-American and Butkus Award winner Trev Alberts received this honor.

569. The first black All-American at Nebraska was also Bob Devaney's first All-American. He was none other than the great Bob Brown, named in 1963.

570. Wayne Meylan was named All-American in both 1966 and 1967. Rich Glover was named All-American in 1971.

571. Tom Heiser, offensive back, became Dr. Tom Heiser in his return as a team physician.

572. Bill "Thunder" Thornton was named in 1961 and played a big part in the success of Bob Devaney's first Husker team in 1962.

573. Dave Rimington was chosen as a center by the Cincinnati Bengals in 1983.

574. In 1984 this gathering celebrated the fact that both Bob Devaney and Tom Osborne had recorded 100 victories at Nebraska. It is believed that they are the only pair to do this back-to-back.

Will Shields

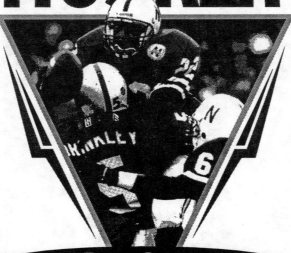

10

HUSKER TRIVIA

BOWL GAMES

575. What was Nebraska's first bowl victory?

576. Who was Nebraska's quarterback in the first Orange Bowl showdown with Alabama after the 1965 season?

577. What was Nebraska's longest bowl game touchdown run and who made it?

578. Why was Nebraska chosen to go to the Orange Bowl after the 1954 season?

579. What was the final play of the 1994 Orange Bowl?

580. In Johnny Rodger's last game as a Husker, against Notre Dame in the 1973 Orange Bowl, for how many touchdowns was he responsible?

581. How many different bowls has Nebraska played in during its long football history?

582. Who holds the N.U. record for the most touchdown passes thrown in a bowl game? How many TD tosses?

575. The first time that the Huskers tasted victory in post-season play was in the 1962 Gotham Bowl when they defeated the Miami (Fla.) Hurricanes 36-34.

576. Bob Churchich played exceedingly well in a 39-28 defeat at the hands of the Crimson Tide. Bob completed 12 of 17 passes for 232 yards and three touchdowns.

577. Amazingly, Dennis Claridge holds the record with a 68 yard scamper in the 1964 Orange Bowl against Auburn.

578. Oklahoma, the Big Seven champion, was ineligible because it had gone to the Orange Bowl the year before. Nebraska was selected because it had finished second in the conference. The final chapter stated that the Huskers were demolished 34-7 by Duke in the Orange Bowl.

579. The last play of the game was a true heartbreaker. Byron Bennett missed a 45 yard field goal attempt with no time left, a kick that would have won a national championship for the Huskers.

580. Rodgers was responsible for 5 scores. He ran for three touchdowns on 15 carries for 81 yards. He caught a 50 yard touchdown pass and also threw a 52 yard TD pass to Frosty Anderson.

581. Nebraska has played in 10 different bowls during its distinguished football history. They have attended the Rose, Sugar, Orange, Cotton, Sun, Liberty, Fiesta, Astro-Bluebonnet, Gotham and Citrus Bowls.

582. Bob Churchich tossed three touchdown passes in a losing effort against Alabama in the 1966 Orange Bowl. The Tide won the game, 39-28. Craig Sundberg tied the record in the 1985 Sugar Bowl game with LSU. The Huskers won the game, 28-10.

583. Who was the All-American quarterback that the Huskers faced in the January 1, 1964 Orange Bowl?

584. Did Nebraska ever lead in the 1984 Orange Bowl against Miami where the "Scoring Explosion" almost captured the national title?

585. Which team did Nebraska play in its only trip to the Astro-Bluebonnet Bowl and after which season did the game take place?

586. Which team prevented Nebraska from setting the NCAA record for most consecutive bowl victories? Which bowl game ended the streak?

587. The 1969 Sun Bowl against Georgia produced a great feat by an N.U. kicker. What was this record?

588. How many times has Nebraska played in the Orange Bowl under Tom Osborne's leadership?

589. What was significant about the two head coaches in the 1994 Orange Bowl and their pursuit of the national championship?

590. What was the longest pass reception in an N.U. bowl game?

591. In what city and stadium was the 1962 Gotham Bowl played?

592. What was Bob Devaney's first bowl game as a head coach?

583. Jimmy Sidle of Auburn proved to be a formidable opponent for the Huskers. He gained 96 yards rushing on 25 carries and completed 12 of 25 passes for another 141 yards. Nebraska won the game by a score of 13-7.

584. No, the Huskers never did catch the Hurricanes after falling behind 17-0 in the first quarter.

585. The Huskers played the Red Raiders of Texas Tech after the 1976 season and defeated them 27-24 to finish the season 9-3-1.

586. Nebraska won 6 straight bowl games before losing to Arizona State 17-14 in the 1975 Fiesta Bowl.

587. Paul Rogers kicked 4 field goals of 50, 32, 42 and 37 yards. They were all kicked in the first quarter of the game!!

588. The Huskers have played in the Orange Bowl nine times with Tom Osborne as head coach. They made it to Miami after the 1978, 1981, 1982, 1983, 1988, 1991, 1992, 1993 and 1994 seasons.

589. Neither Tom Osborne of Nebraska nor Bobby Bowden of Florida State had won a national title. In this game, with the teams ranked 1 and 2, there was no way that one of them could avoid getting the monkey off his back.

590. Jerry Tagge tossed a 56 yard pass to Johnny Rodgers in the 1972 Orange Bowl against Alabama.

591. The ill-fated Gotham Bowl was played in New York City in Yankee Stadium.

592. His first bowl game was the 1959 Sun Bowl in which his Wyoming Cowboys defeated Hardin-Simmons by a score of 14-6.

593. Which Nebraska coach has taken his team to the most bowl games?

594. What was unusual about the 1977 Liberty Bowl game program?

595. Who scored the winning points in the thrilling come-from-behind Sugar Bowl victory over Florida in 1974?

596. Who came off the bench in the 1977 Liberty Bowl against North Carolina and led the Huskers to a 21-17 victory?

597. What great quarterback faced the Huskers in the Gotham Bowl of 1962?

598. In 1980 the Huskers defeated Mississippi State 31-17 in the Sun Bowl. This was a return visit to El Paso. When was the last time the Huskers had played in the Sun Bowl?

599. In nine straight bowl games for Nebraska from 1986 through the 1994 Orange Bowl, on the average, who ranked higher, the Huskers or their opponents?

593. Tom Osborne has taken the Huskers to 22 straight bowl games, 1973-1994. Every team that he has fielded has played in a bowl game.

594. On the cover of the program was none other than the "King," Memphis' own, Elvis Presley. Nebraska defeated North Carolina in the game 21-17 with a furious fourth quarter comeback.

595. Mike Coyle tied the game 10-10 in the fourth quarter with a field goal and then won the contest by kicking another three-pointer with only 1:46 left in the game.

596. Quarterback Randy Garcia threw a fourth quarter 34-yard touchdown pass to Tim Smith to secure the Husker victory. He had earlier tossed a 10-yard scoring pass to Curtis Craig. Garcia had come in to relieve starter Tom Sorley. Nebraska had trailed by as much as 17-7 going into the fourth quarter of the game. Garcia completed all 3 of his pass attempts for 56 yards and two touchdowns.

597. George Mira of Miami of Florida was superb in a losing effort. He completed 24 of 46 passes for 321 yards and two touchdowns.

598. In 1969 Nebraska met Georgia in the Sun Bowl and demolished the Bulldogs 45-6.

599. For nine straight years all of Nebraska's bowl opponents had ranked higher than the Huskers and all had been among the top five in the nation. This explained Nebraska's bowl difficulties that ended with the 1995 Orange Bowl victory.

600. What passing combination in the January 1, 1966 Orange Bowl crushed Nebraska's hopes for a victory over Alabama?

601. What was the greatest number of pass interceptions made by the Huskers in a bowl game?

602. Who was the Clemson middle guard who bragged that he would "handle" Outland Trophy winner Dave Rimington in the 1982 Orange Bowl?

603. Between 1983 and 1987 Nebraska played the same team in a bowl game three years out of five. Who was this team?

604. Dennis Claridge set a major game record in the 1964 Orange Bowl game against Auburn. What was this record?

605. The quarterback who engineered Nebraska's crushing 39-28 defeat in the 1966 Orange Bowl faced the Huskers as coach of their opponents in the 1976 Astro-Bluebonnet Bowl. Who was he?

606. How many different bowl games has Nebraska played in since Tom Osborne has become head coach of the Huskers?

607. In the 1973 Orange Bowl game against Notre Dame, how many of Nebraska's 40 points was Johnny Rodgers responsible for?

600. The combination of Steve Sloan to Ray Perkins proved to be too much for the Huskers. Sloan completed 20 of 28 passes for 296 yards and two touchdowns. Perkins had 9 receptions for 159 yards and two scores.

601. Nebraska defenders picked off 6 Georgia Bulldog passes in the 1969 Sun Bowl. The Huskers won the game 45-6.

602. Freshman William "Refrigerator" Perry was the one who was handled. He didn't make a tackle in the game, a 22-15 Clemson victory.

603. The Huskers played LSU in the 1983 Orange Bowl and the 1985 and 1987 Sugar Bowls. Nebraska won all three contests.

604. Claridge made a 68 yard touchdown run on the second play of the game. At the time it was the longest run from scrimmage in the history of the Orange Bowl and a very unlikely record for a quarterback to establish.

605. Steve Sloan was in his second year as coach of Texas Tech when his team was defeated 27-24 by Nebraska.

606. The Huskers have played in eight different bowl games, 1973-94. They played in the Cotton Bowl after the 1973 and 1979 seasons, the Sugar Bowl after the 1974, 1984 and 1986 seasons, the Fiesta Bowl after the 1975, 1985, 1987 and 1989 seasons, the Astro-Bluebonnet Bowl after the 1976 season, the Liberty Bowl after the 1977 season, the Sun Bowl after the 1980 season, the Florida Citrus Bowl after the 1990 season, and, of course, the Orange Bowl after the 1978, 1981, 1982, 1983, 1988, 1991, 1992, 1993 and 1994 seasons.

607. The great Heisman Trophy winner was responsible for 30 points as he scored on three touchdown runs, caught a TD pass and threw a scoring pass to Frosty Anderson.

608. In the 1988 Sunkist Fiesta Bowl this Florida State quarterback shattered his personal best for passing yards by 100 yards and almost single-handedly crushed the Husker's hopes. Name this Seminole.

609. Who coached Nebraska's two bowl teams before the Devaney era?

610. Who was the great Stanford T-formation quarterback that faced N.U. in the 1941 Rose Bowl?

611. Which player holds the N.U. school record for the most points scored in a bowl game?

612. Bob Churchich tied an Orange Bowl record in the 1966 classic. What was the record that he tied?

613. Though Nebraska was #1 going into the 1994 Orange Bowl against #2 Florida State, they were underdogs. By how many points was State favored?

614. In the 1974 Sugar Bowl against Florida, who led the Huskers to a 13-10 victory after Dave Humm could not get the team moving?

615. Who was the star running back that Nebraska defenders hogtied in Osborne's first bowl game as a head coach?

616. Who scored the winning touchdown in the 1971 Orange Bowl, a 17-12 victory over LSU? This famous touchdown, the subject of many photos and posters, gave Nebraska its first national championship.

608. Danny McManus was unstoppable that day, throwing for 375 yards and three touchdown passes in a 31-28 Florida State victory.

609. Biff Jones led the 1941 Rose Bowl team and Bill Glassford was the coach of the 1955 Orange Bowl team.

610. Frankie Albert, the great Stanford quarterback, led his team to a hard-fought 21-13 victory.

611. Johnny Rodgers scored 24 points against Notre Dame in his 1973 Orange Bowl. He had three touchdown runs and one touchdown reception.

612. Churchich threw three touchdown passes in the game. Unfortunately, he threw them in a losing effort against Alabama. The Tide won the game handily, 39-28.

613. The point spread, 17 1/2 was an insult to Nebraska fans and a great motivator. It was believed to be the largest point spread ever in which a top ranked team has been an underdog.

614. Junior Terry Luck came off the bench with the Gators ahead 10-0 and led the Huskers to a touchdown and two field goals late in the contest.

615. In the 1974 Cotton Bowl the renowned Roosevelt Leaks from Texas was held to only 48 yards in 19-3 Husker victory. Leaks had earlier finished 3rd in the 1973 Heisman Trophy balloting.

616. Jerry Tagge stretched his arms over the goal line from one yard out. As the ball broke the plane of the goal, probably most the state of Nebraska cheered as one.

617. In which year did the Huskers play in the Liberty Bowl and against which team did they play?

618. In the 1990 Sunkist Fiesta Bowl a Florida State quarterback threw for 422 yards and 5 scores. Who was this player?

619. In the 1959 Sun Bowl in which Devaney's Wyoming team defeated Hardin-Simmons, who was the opposing head coach? (Hint - he was one of the all-time great NFL quarterbacks.)

620. Who had Nebraska's longest punt return in a bowl game?

621. What bowl did N.U. go to in 1973, the first season with Tom Osborne as head coach?

622. How many times did Nebraska go to the Orange Bowl under the leadership of Bob Devaney?

623. In the 1993 Federal Express Orange Bowl, 7 turnovers contributed to Nebraska's 27-14 loss to Florida State. What is ironic about these turnovers?

624. Which Nebraska player was the offensive player of the 1974 Cotton Bowl and also the 1974 Sugar Bowl (which was played on New Year's Eve)?

625. Which Alabama receiver game Nebraska defenders fits in the 1966 Orange Bowl game, a 39-28 Tide victory? He later went on to greatness in the NFL and then returned to the college ranks as a coach.

617. Nebraska played against North Carolina in the 1977 Liberty Bowl and won a hard-fought game 21-17.

618. Peter Tom Willis had a phenomenal day, setting the record for passing totals allowed to a Nebraska opponent. Willis broke the previous record of 375 yards set two years earlier by another Seminole, Danny McManus, in the 1988 Sunkist Fiesta Bowl.

619. Slingin' Sammy Baugh, formerly of the Washington Redskins, matched wits with Bob Devaney that day in 1959.

620. Johnny Rodgers returned a punt 77 yards for a touchdown against Alabama in the 1972 Orange Bowl.

621. The Huskers played in the Cotton Bowl after the 1973 season. The result was a 19-3 Husker victory over Texas in Dallas.

622. The Huskers were invited to play in the Orange Bowl 5 times under Devaney's leadership, after the following seasons: 1963, 1965, 1970, 1971 and 1972.

623. The Huskers had only had 12 turnovers during the entire season and led the nation in turnover margin with a +18 record.

624. "Tough" Tony Davis was honored both times for his inspirational play in these bowl games. In the Cotton Bowl, Davis gained 106 yards on 28 carries and scored one touchdown. In the Sugar Bowl Tony gained 126 tough yards on 17 carries.

625. Ray Perkins caught 9 passes for 159 yards and two touchdowns against the Huskers in the Orange Bowl. He returned to Alabama to take over as head coach in 1983 after the great Bear Bryant stepped down.

626. Who holds the N.U. school record for the longest field goal in a bowl game?

627. Bob Devaney's teams went to bowl games in his first five years at Nebraska. What bowls did his teams attend?

628. Nebraska played in the first night bowl game. What was it?

629. Which bowl victory propelled Nebraska to its first national championship?

630. The 1941 Rose Bowl team was truly Nebraska's representative. Of the team's 39 members, how many were native Nebraskans?

631. Why was there a delay in leaving for the Gotham Bowl in 1962?

632. How many consecutive bowls has Nebraska played in up to the present time?

633. Two huskers switched jerseys in the 1984 Orange Bowl to confuse Miami quarterback, Bernie Kosar. Who were they?

626. Paul Rogers booted a 50 yarder against Georgia in the 1969 Sun Bowl. He had four three-pointers that day, all in the first quarter. Gregg Barrios tied the record with a 50 yarder of his one against Miami in the 1989 Orange Bowl. Those were the only points that Nebraska scored.

627. The Huskers went to the Gotham Bowl in 1962, the Orange Bowl after the 1963 season, the Cotton Bowl after the 1964 season, the Orange Bowl after the 1965 season and the Sugar Bowl after the 1966 season.

628. The Huskers met the Alabama Crimson Tide in the 1966 Orange Bowl, the first night bowl game. Unfortunately, they lost the game, 39-28.

629. The January 1, 1971 Orange Bowl, a 17-12 victory over LSU, plus some timely upsets of teams rated above Nebraska, gave the Huskers their first national title.

630. On the team 38 of 39 were natives of the great state of Nebraska. In later years it became increasingly difficult to compete successfully without extensive recruiting outside of Nebraska.

631. The N.U. coaches waited until the bowl payment check was put on deposit in New York to cover the expenses, so shaky was the Gotham Bowl's financial condition.

632. The Huskers have appeared in 26 straight bowl games from 1969 to 1994. Tom Osborne's teams have played in a bowl game each of his 22 years as head coach at Nebraska.

633. They were defensive players Dave Burke and Mike McCashland. The ploy was not totally successful as Miami still netted 300 yards passing in a 31-30 victory.

634. Who quarterbacked the Husker team to its 22-15 loss to Clemson in the 1982 Orange Bowl?

635. When the Huskers faced Mississippi State in the 1980 Sun Bowl, they faced a coach who had earlier produced an offense that had haunted Nebraska for years. Who was this coach and what offense did he create?

636. What was so remarkable about the manner in which Terry Luck led Nebraska to a thrilling come-from-behind win over Florida in the 1974 Sugar Bowl?

637. With Nebraska's appearance in the 1995 Orange Bowl, they set the NCAA record for consecutive bowl trips. Whose record did they surpass?

638. How many different bowl games did Nebraska play in while Bob Devaney was the head coach?

639. When Johnny Rodgers received the Orange Bowl game ball after Nebraska had crushed Alabama in the January 1, 1972 classic, to whom did he give the ball in a very emotional moment?

640. Who shredded Nebraska's pass defenses in a 34-7 Husker loss in the January 1, 1967 Sugar Bowl?

634. Mark Mauer took over for Turner Gill who had injured his right leg in the Iowa State game. Unfortunately, Mauer was not able to duplicate the success that he enjoyed in the Oklahoma game as Gill's replacement. He was 5 for 15 in passing for 38 yards and gained a net 10 yards rushing.

635. Emory Bellard, the Bulldog coach, had developed the wishbone offense in 1968 while he was an assistant coach at Texas. Oklahoma later refined the wishbone into an utterly awesome weapon.

636. He led the Huskers to a 13-10 victory without completing a single pass. Luck was 0 for 2 in replacing Dave Humm who was 2 for 14 passing for 16 yards and 4 interceptions. Luckily, the Huskers rushed for more than 300 yards in the game.

637. Nebraska erased Alabama's record of 25 straight bowl appearances, 1959-1983. The Huskers have gone bowling every year since the 1969 Sun Bowl.

638. The Huskers played in 5 different bowl games, the Gotham Bowl in 1962, the Cotton Bowl in 1964, the Sugar Bowl after the 1966 season, the Sun Bowl after the 1969 season and the Orange Bowl after the 1963, 1965, 1970, 1971 and 1972 seasons.

639. Rodgers, without hesitation, gave the game ball to Rex Lowe, an N.U. split end, who was stricken by Hodgkins Disease.

640. Kenny "The Snake" Stabler, who won the game MVP award, led Alabama to an overwhelming victory. The future All-Pro quarterback completed 12 of 18 passes for 218 yards and one touchdown. Ray Perkins hauled in 7 passes for 178 yards and one score.

641. Who was the great quarterback that the Huskers faced in the 1971 Orange Bowl, a 17-12 victory which sealed N.U.'s first national championship? He was later a very successful NFL quarterback.

642. In how many consecutive New Year's Day bowl games has Nebraska played, counting the 1995 Orange Bowl appearance?

641. The Huskers faced Bert Jones of LSU. He gave Nebraska everything he had, but the Huskers held on for the victory and the championship.

642. Through the 1995 Orange Bowl the Huskers have played in 14 straight New Year's Day bowls dating back to the 1980 Sun Bowl where they defeated Mississippi State, 31-17, on December 27, 1980.

Byron Bennett & Mike Stigge

11

BIG EIGHT RIVALRIES

643. In 1965, against Oklahoma State, with N.U. ahead 21-17 and time running out, which great runner almost won the game for the Cowboys?

644. Devaney's team faced Gale Sayers and his Jayhawk teammates three times. How did Kansas fare during those years against the Huskers?

645. Who almost had Johnny Rodgers before he got started on his famous 72 yard punt return in the Game of the Century in 1971?

646. When was the last season that Tom Osborne faced his old nemesis, Barry Switzer, on the football field?

647. Kelly Phelps started as quarterback for the Sooners when N.U. and Oklahoma met in 1982. He had an inauspicious debut to the series in 1978. What happened to him?

648. Nebraska finished number 1 in the polls in 1971 and 1994. What was similar about Colorado's ranking in those seasons?

649. Who was the Kansas State quarterback who guided the Wildcats to their stunning 12-0 shutout of the Huskers in 1968? He later made quite a name for himself in the NFL.

650. When Colorado finally defeated Nebraska 20-12 in 1986, how lengthy was the Husker win streak in the series?

651. What was the most points scored by a Big Eight opponent in Memorial Stadium?

643. Walt Garrison, later of Dallas Cowboy fame, ran the last play of the game from N.U.'s 23 to the 5 yard line before being tackled by Billy Johnson. He gained 121 yards on 19 carries that day.

644. Sayers never tasted victory against Devaney's Huskers during his playing days at Kansas. The Jayhawks lost 40-16 in 1962, 23-9 in 1963 and 14-7 in 1964.

645. His old rival, Greg Pruitt, slipped off of Rodgers right after Johnny took the punt. The rest, as they say, is history.

646. Switzer, who grew weary of the media strain and fan pressure, decided to resign after the 1988 season. He owned a 12-5 edge over Osborne.

647. Phelps was the freshman return man who was absolutely leveled on a kickoff in the 2nd half of the 1978 game. The ball was fumbled but the officials ruled that Phelps was down when he lost the ball. Nebraska still won the game, 17-14.

648. Ironically, the Buffaloes ended up No.3 in 1971 and matched that ranking in 1994.

649. Lynn Dickey and running back Mack Herron helped bring about one of Devaney's most disheartening losses as Nebraska's head coach. Dickey later played for a number of teams in the NFL.

650. The Huskers had won 18 straight contests with the Buffaloes, dating back to a 1967 21-16 loss in Lincoln.

651. Oklahoma scored 48 points against the Huskers in 1949 to establish the stadium record.

652. Who made the crunching hit on the kickoff returner in the 1978 Oklahoma game that produced a fumble which was wrongfully blown dead?

653. Out of the last 31 games with Oklahoma how many times has the winning team had to come from behind to secure the victory?

654. Since Bob Devaney's arrival at Nebraska, how many times has Oklahoma spoiled N.U.'s perfect season hopes?

655. Question----What happened to Nebraska after the Huskers defeated a ranked Kansas State team in its championship run in 1994?

656. In 1970, when N.U. crushed Kansas State 51-13, the Huskers intercepted the Wildcat quarterback seven times. He later went on to bigger things in the NFL. Who was he?

657. When the Huskers lost to Iowa State, 19-10, in 1992, Nebraska's win streak against the Cyclones was broken. How many consecutive wins did Nebraska have in the series?

658. In a 1961 home game against Colorado, the Huskers produced a most embarrassing statistic. What was it?

659. In 1892 Missouri forfeited a game to Nebraska. Why?

652. This hit has been shown many times in highlight films. Linebacker John Ruud, who lettered 1978-79, nailed Kelly Phelps and knocked him silly on the play. Ruud's brother, Tom, was an All-American Husker linebacker.

653. So many of these contests have been seesaw affairs with the outcome in doubt until the very end. The eventual winner has had to come from behind 24 out of 31 games (through 1994).

654. The Sooners handed the Huskers their first season loss five times, in 1964, 1966, 1975, 1979 and 1987.

655. Unbelievably, the Huskers dropped from 2nd to 3rd after they defeated the 11th ranked Wildcats in Manhattan.

656. Lynn Dickey was the signal caller that the Blackshirts plagued that day. He later went on to glory with the Green Bay Packers.

657. Before the 1992 debacle in Ames, Nebraska had not lost to Iowa State since a 24-21 setback in 1977, a 14 year win streak.

658. Unbelievably, in the light of the Huskers' recent offensive might, Nebraska was unable to muster even a single first down against the Buffaloes that day. N.U. failed to complete one pass that cold November day and had a dismal 31 net yards in total offense in a 7-0 shutout loss.

659. Missouri forfeited the game because Nebraska had a black running back by the name of George Flippin on the team and the Tigers refused to play them because of that fact.

660. What was the biggest margin of victory for Nebraska for a Big Eight game played at Memorial Stadium?

661. What is the longest win string versus Big Eight teams that Nebraska has enjoyed at Memorial Stadium?

662. Gale Sayers, the great running back, almost attended N.U. but opted to play at Kansas. Which Nebraska high school did Sayers attend?

663. When Nebraska lost to Missouri 17-7 in 1962, how many years had it been since the Huskers had scored a touchdown against the Tigers?

664. Who was the little-known Iowa State quarterback who almost single-handedly produced the 19-10 Cyclone upset of Nebraska in 1992?

665. The 1963 game against Oklahoma had some external distractions. What had happened?

666. In 1964, against Iowa State, what important injury affected N.U.'s play the rest of the season?

667. The 1993 televised game against Oklahoma State was turned by a single play made by Barron Miles, a Husker defensive back. What was this extraordinary play?

668. What happened to Missouri the week after the Huskers destroyed them 62-0 in 1972?

660. The largest victory margin was the 62-0 demolition of Missouri in 1972.

661. Nebraska won 15 straight games against Big Eight teams in the confines of Memorial Stadium, 1962-67.

662. Gale graduated from Omaha Central High. He went on to great fame with the Chicago Bears.

663. Believe it or not, the Huskers had last scored a touchdown against Missouri in a 14-13 loss in 1957, five years earlier. Missouri had shut out Nebraska 4 straight years, from 1958-61.

664. Marv Seiler was almost unstoppable, rushing for 144 yards on 24 carries and setting up 4 field goals and a touchdown. It was perhaps the biggest upset of the year.

665. President Kennedy had been assassinated the day before, on Friday, November 22. It was only after a six hour meeting that the Nebraska regents decided to let the game go on as scheduled.

666. Quarterback Fred Duda was carried from the field in the first quarter with a broken leg. A sophomore, Bob Churchich, took over for the rest of the season and Huskers won 6 of the next 7 games in 1964.

667. On perhaps the defensive play of the year, Miles blocked a Cowboy punt in the end zone with the score tied 13-13 in the 4th quarter. Miles caught the ball in mid-air and scored the touchdown. Nebraska went on to win the game 27-13.

668. The very next week the roller coaster Tigers defeated 8th ranked and previously undefeated Notre Dame 30-26 at South Bend.

669. Name the only Big Eight team that has not defeated Nebraska since the arrival of Bob Devaney in 1962.

670. Which crucial Husker defensive player was knocked out of the game early in the first quarter of the 1993 Oklahoma game?

671. Who ran the pitchout for 43 yards to set up Oklahoma's winning touchdown with time running out in the 1980 show-down? His run snatched victory from the jaws of defeat for the Sooners.

672. What was the pivotal play in the 1976 34-24 loss to Missouri?

673. Since the beginning of the Devaney-Osborne era, what was Nebraska's biggest margin of victory over its arch-rival, Oklahoma? When did the victory take place?

674. How many lead changes were there in the 1971 Game of the Century?

675. What was distinctive about Thomas Lott's apparel when he played quarterback at Oklahoma and plagued the Huskers?

676. After the thrilling 17-14 victory over Oklahoma in 1978, what happened at Memorial Stadium for only the second time in its history?

677. In the 1982 Missouri game an injury to an N.U. player caused an enormous controversy and almost cost the Huskers the game. What happened?

669. Oklahoma State has come close several times but the best they could muster during the 32 years is a 17-17 tie with the Huskers in 1973, Osborne's first season as head coach at N.U.

670. Things looked really bleak when Butkus Award winner Trev Alberts dislocated his elbow very early in the game. The Huskers had to claw their way back from a deficit to post a 21-7 victory.

671. Buster "The Man With Luster" Rhymes, a slick freshman running back, delivered the crushing blow to the Huskers. He later scored from the one to ice the game for Oklahoma, a 21-17 Sooner victory.

672. Pete Woods threw a desperation pass from his own end zone to Joe Stewart. The end result was a 98 yard touchdown. Nebraska had led 24-23 and went on to lose 34-24.

673. Perhaps one of Nebraska's sweetest victories was the 30 point crushing of the Sooners, 44-14 in 1969.

674. There were a total of four lead changes in this superlative contest.

675. Many times N.U. fans saw one of Lott's colorful bandannas flowing in the breeze from underneath his helmet. He wore them to protect his afro hairdo.

676. The goal posts were torn down, pieces of which were paraded through the streets of Lincoln by joyous Husker fans.

677. Turner Gill was pushed by Tiger Randy Jostes in the second quarter. He suffered a mild concussion when he hit the ground and could not return to action. The Huskers rallied in the fourth quarter to win 23-19 in a very tight contest.

678. In the 1971 Game of the Century, which team was more effective passing the football?

679. When was Kansas State's last victory over Nebraska?

680. In the 1974 Oklahoma game, the Huskers pulled ahead of the Sooners 14-7 with a very unusual touchdown. How did they do it?

681. Which Big Eight teams have never defeated the Huskers since Tom Osborne took over as head coach in 1973?

682. Even though Jeff Kinney gained 171 yards in the Game of the Century, how long was his longest touchdown run?

683. In the 1968 47-0 loss to Oklahoma, which Sooner back had a tremendous afternoon against the Huskers?

684. When Nebraska upset Oklahoma in 1959 how many consecutive games had the Sooners played without a loss?

685. When was the last time that Kansas defeated Nebraska?

686. Which Oklahoma Sooner tight end rumbled for an end around touchdown run in the annual showdown in 1985? (Hint—he later played for the Philadelphia Eagles and, most recently, the Miami Dolphins.)

678. As a wishbone team Oklahoma was a surprise passing threat against Nebraska. Jack Mildren threw for 137 yards and Jerry Tagge only managed 65 yards. That's over a 2 to 1 advantage.

679. The last time the Wildcats accomplished this feat was the 12-0 shocker in 1968, the second of Devaney's two 6-4-0 seasons at Nebraska.

680. Quarterback David Humm pitched the ball back to John O'Leary who then dropped back and passed the ball to Humm who went in from the Sooner 11 yard line.

681. Three teams, namely Kansas, Kansas State and Oklahoma State have never claimed a victory against Tom Osborne's troops in his 22-year tenure at Nebraska.

682. Kinney did most of his damage getting into scoring position. His longest touchdown run was only three yards.

683. Steve Owens, winner of the 1969 Heisman Trophy, ran for 172 yards and scored 5 touchdowns in Devaney's worst defeat in 11 years as coach of the Huskers. It was N.U.'s most lopsided defeat since the Sooner's crushing of Nebraska 54-6 in 1956.

684. Oklahoma had gone 75 games without a loss, dating back to November 9, 1946 when the Kansas Jayhawks had beaten the Sooners 16-13.

685. The Jayhawks last accomplished this feat in 1968 when Kansas tied for the Big Eight title. Kansas won the game 23-13 and Nebraska finished the season 6-4-0 in 1968, a definite off-season for the Huskers.

686. Keith Jackson shocked Husker fans with an 88 yard touchdown gallop in a 27-7 Sooner victory.

NU vs. OU

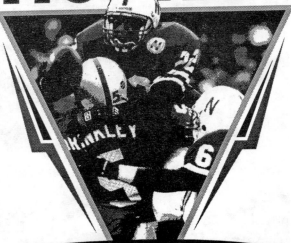

HUSKER TRIVIA

12

Non-Conference Rivals

687. Who played in the first Kickoff Classic in 1983?

688. When Washington State upset the Huskers in 1977, their quarterback gave Nebraska fits. He later went on to play in the NFL for the Cincinnati Bengals and the Tampa Bay Buccaneers. Who was this player?

689. In the first game of 1955, Nebraska suffered one of its most embarrassing defeats. What happened?

690. In 1979 when the series with Iowa resumed, who came off the bench to spark a comeback 24-21 victory when I.M. Hipp was felled by an injury?

691. The quarterback who led UCLA to the stunning upset of Nebraska in 1972, 20-17, ending the Husker's 23 game winning streak, was the son of one of the greatest football players of all time. Who was he?

692. What was Bob Devaney's record against his old nemesis, Bear Bryant of Alabama?

693. When Northern Illinois played Nebraska in 1989 and 1990, there was a direct coaching link with the Huskers. What was the connection?

687. Nebraska defeated the Penn State Nittany Lions in the inaugural Kickoff Classic. The score, 44-6, truly reflected a Husker blowout. Nebraska went on to hold the number 1 ranking in the polls the entire season, until the disappointment in Miami.

688. He was none other than the "Throwin' Samoan" Jack Thompson. The Cougar quarterback completed 18 of 30 passes for 174 yards and two touchdowns to pace Washington State to a 19-10 upset victory over the Huskers.

689. This astounding loss was the 6-0 setback to Hawaii, a team that the Huskers had crushed only the season before, 50-0. To be shut out by a lightweight like Hawaii was certainly one of the most shocking and humiliating failures endured by the football programs during the Forgettable Fifties.

690. Craig Johnson, a junior who had expected to be redshirted by Osborne, teamed with quarterback sub Tim Hager to bring the Huskers back from the brink of disaster.

691. He was Mark Harmon, son of old number 98, Tom Harmon from Michigan. N.U. also had a string of 32 games without a defeat snapped by Harmon and his friends. Harmon later found fame in acting.

692. Bob was 1-2-0 against the Bear. Devaney's Huskers lost to Alabama, 39-28 in the 1966 Orange Bowl and 34-7 in the 1967 Sugar Bowl. He got some sweet revenge in the 1972 Orange Bowl when the Huskers crushed the Tide, 38-6.

693. Jerry Pettibone, a former Nebraska assistant coach and recruiting coordinator, was the Northern Illinois head coach. The Huskers demolished Pettibone's team 48-17 in 1989 and 60-14 in 1990.

694. How many times has Nebraska played Hawaii under Tom Osborne's leadership?

695. Nebraska had a tremendous game in 1925 against mighty Illinois and Red Grange. How did Grange fare against the Huskers?

696. What was the biggest victory margin for the Huskers in a non-conference game played in Memorial Stadium?

697. What was the largest crowd at Memorial Stadium for a non-conference opponent?

698. In 1982 Nebraska almost suffered a tremendous upset at Hawaii. Which important player was unable to play in the first half and why?

699. In 1962, when N.U. defeated its three non-conference foes, how long had it been since the Huskers could boast of defeating all of its non-conference opponents?

700. In 1992 and 1993 Nebraska faced two Division 1-AA opponents. Prior to 1992, when was the last time that the Huskers had faced a non-Division 1-A team?

694. The Huskers have played the Rainbows three times under Tom Osborne, 1976 in Hawaii with Nebraska winning 68-3, 1978 in Lincoln with Nebraska winning 56-10 and 1982 in Hawaii with Huskers pulling away to a 37-16 victory.

695. Remarkably, the awesome Grange was held to very few yards by the swarming Husker defense and Illinois lost 14-0 to Nebraska. It was one of Nebraska's greatest victories and one of Grange's most frustrating games. This game helped to establish Nebraska's reputation as a formidable football power.

696. The biggest blowout for a home non-conference game was the 68-0 pasting given to New Mexico State when it visited Memorial Stadium in 1982. The Huskers set several NCAA offensive records that day.

697. The record was established in 1983 when 76,510 fans filled Memorial Stadium to watch the Huskers defeat UCLA 42-10.

698. Quarterback Turner Gill was unable to play because of severe back spasms. He led Nebraska to a furious fourth quarter comeback that resulted in a 37-16 victory.

699. The Huskers had not dispatched all of their non-conference foes since the great 1915 team had accomplished the feat some 47 years earlier.

700. Playing Middle Tennessee State and North Texas State did little to improve public perception of Nebraska's schedule strength. The Huskers had not faced a non-Division I-A opponents since South Dakota in 1964.

701. During the mediocre 1968 season, Nebraska pulled out victories in the last 2 minutes against Wyoming and Minnesota in the same manner. How did the Huskers win these games?

702. Who heroically continued to play in the 1974 loss to Wisconsin even after his jaw broken?

703. In Bob Devaney's eleven years as head coach of the Huskers, his teams lost only three non-conference regular season games. Who beat Nebraska and when?

704. In 1980 when Florida State pulled off an 18-14 upset at Memorial Stadium, Nebraska almost salvaged a victory. What play broke the Huskers' backs as they were driving for the go-ahead score?

705. Before Nebraska and Iowa renewed their rivalry in 1979, when was the last time that two teams had faced each other?

706. When Washington State upset the Huskers in Lincoln in 1977, who was their head coach and where did he move to in the next season?

707. In 1984 Syracuse pulled off a huge upset of Nebraska in the Carrier Dome. What was it about the 1983 game that made this result an even greater shock?

708. How many times did Devaney's N.U. teams face service academy schools, 1962-72?

701. Paul Rogers won both games with a field goal, a 51 yarder against Wyoming with 21 seconds left and a 19 yarder against Minnesota with 92 seconds left. The difficulties in defeating these less than feared opponents foretold problems with the season's later games.

702. John O'Leary received a broken jaw and several broken teeth in the first half. He still managed to gain 88 yards on 17 carries. Nebraska lost the game 21-20 on a 77 yard pass by Wisconsin at the end of the game.

703. The Huskers were defeated 17-13 in 1963 by Air Force, 31-21 by Southern California in 1969 and 20-17 by UCLA in 1972.

704. Jeff Quinn, the Husker quarterback, was on the Seminole 3 yard line with 10 seconds left in the game when the ball was stripped from his hands. The ball was recovered by Florida State and Nebraska's victory hopes were dashed.

705. The last time Nebraska and Iowa met was in 1946 and Iowa was a 21-7 victor.

706. Warren Powers was the head coach of the Washington State team in 1977 and in 1978 he became the coach of the Missouri Tigers who then upset the Huskers that year. Powers and Osborne had both been assistants at Nebraska under Bob Devaney.

707. The Triplets had absolutely crushed the Orangemen in 1983, 63-7, so Husker fans were totally unprepared for the 1984 debacle.

708. The Huskers faced service teams four times. Against Air Force N.U. lost 17-13 in 1963 and won 27-17 in 1965. Against Army Nebraska won 28-0 in 1970 and 77-7 in 1972.

709. Nebraska lost to Miami of Florida 31-30 in the 1984 Orange Bowl. The last time that Nebraska had faced Miami in 1976, Miami had a Nebraska connection. What was it?

710. In 1977, against Alabama, in a 31-24 victory, Nebraska scored its first touchdown on a very gutsy call by Tom Osborne. What was the play that he called?

711. Who was Nebraska's first opponent after Bob Devaney took over as coach in 1962?

712. Tom Osborne has lost to only three Big Ten teams in his 21 years as head coach at Nebraska. Which teams defeated the Huskers and during which seasons did the losses occur?

713. A true freshman running back came off the bench to perform spectacularly in the 1993 UCLA game. Who is this player?

709. The head coach of the Hurricanes was Carl Selmer, who had been an assistant coach under Bob Devaney. Selmer had come with Devaney from Wyoming to Nebraska in 1962. Though the Huskers defeated Selmer's Hurricanes in 1975 and 1976, both games were hard fought, difficult Nebraska victories.

710. Instead of going for a safe field goal to bring the score to 7-6, Osborne called for a fake and Randy Garcia passed 7 yards to Rick Berns for the touchdown to put the Huskers ahead 10-7.

711. The Huskers crushed South Dakota, 53-0, in a very impressive debut on September 22, 1962.

712. Wisconsin defeated Nebraska 21-20 in 1974, Iowa beat the Huskers 10-7 in 1981 and Michigan outscored Nebraska 27-23 in the 1986 Fiesta Bowl.

713. Lawrence Phillips was not only a true freshman but he grew up 30 minutes from the Rose Bowl. He and Tommie Frazier saved the Huskers in a 14-13 victory. Phillips gained 137 tough yards on 28 carries and scored one touchdown.

Neil Smith

13

MISCELLANY

714. What was the last conference title that Nebraska won before Bob Devaney took over as head coach in 1962?

715. What was Nebraska's longest winning streak?

716. In a composite of all 22 final AP polls since Tom Osborne became head coach in 1973, how high does Nebraska rank?

717. To which conference did Nebraska belong before the Big Six came into being?

718. Which of Nebraska's football opponents has played the Huskers the most times?

719. What was Nebraska's last undefeated and untied team, including bowl game, before the 1971 national championship team?

720. Nebraska has overall done well on television. On which network have the Huskers had the most success?

721. Nebraska holds the NCAA record for consecutive home sellouts. How many have the Huskers recorded?

722. What was the most home games won in a season by Nebraska?

723. At which game did Nebraska play before the largest crowd?

714. Unbelievably, the last time that Nebraska won a conference title before the arrival of Bob Devaney was in 1940, the Rose Bowl season, when the Huskers took the Big Six crown.

715. The Huskers had a winning streak of 27 games from 1901 to 1904.

716. Although the Huskers have won only one national championship in 22 years, they have done so consistently well in the polls that they are the overall leader.

717. The Huskers were members of the Missouri Valley Conference before six teams decided to form a new conference in 1928. The Huskers won the first Big Six football title in that season.

718. Kansas has played the Huskers a grand total of 101 times for the all-time record.

719. The last team to finish all of its games with an unblemished record was the 1915 powerhouse of Jumbo Stiehm which ended with a record of 8-0-0.

720. Nebraska wishes it could play all of its televised games on ESPN. The Huskers have a record of 19-3-1 on ESPN through 1994.

721. The Huskers have recorded 201 consecutive sellouts from 1962 through the end of the 1994 season.

722. The Huskers have won 7 home games in 1971, 1975, 1989 and 1993.

723. The record was established at the January 1, 1941 Rose Bowl which was attended by 92,000 people.

724. When was the last time that Nebraska was left off of the Associated Press college football poll?

725. What was the last game that Nebraska lost before it won the national championship in 1970?

726. What is Nebraska's longest unbeaten streak?

727. Nebraska has had 33 consecutive winning seasons. Which team ranks second in this category?

728. In what season was the first "Band Day" held in Memorial Stadium?

729. What was the first game lost by Nebraska after it had won its second consecutive national championship in 1971?

730. Nebraska has posted 26 consecutive seasons with at least nine wins. Which team ranks second in this category?

731. In what year was Nebraska first ranked in the final UPI poll?

732. What was N.U.'s longest winning streak at Memorial Stadium?

733. When was the last time that Nebraska lost a homecoming game?

724. The Huskers have been included in every AP poll since early in the 1981 season.

725. Nebraska lost to the Missouri Tigers 17-7 in the fourth game of the 1969 season. They did not lose again until the first game of the 1972 season.

726. The Huskers had an unbeaten streak of 34 games from 1912 to 1916.

727. Nebraska's old rival, Oklahoma, ranks second in consecutive winning seasons with 29 through 1994. In contrast, Florida State has 18 and Miami has only 15.

728. Band Day, a venerable tradition at Memorial Stadium, was first held in 1939 with 10 high school bands invited to play.

729. The Huskers lost the first game of the 1972 season, a 20-17 shocker to the UCLA Bruins. That loss put a serious crimp in Bob Devaney's dreams of winning a third consecutive championship.

730. Miami of Florida is a distant second with 10 consecutive seasons with nine or more victories.

731. In 1963, Nebraska finished 5th in the season finale ratings after a 9-1-0 regular season record.

732. Nebraska won 23 straight games in Memorial Stadium, 1969-72.

733. The Huskers have not lost a homecoming game since they were humiliated (and shut out) by lowly Kansas State, 12-0, in 1968. Since then there have been 26 straight homecoming victories.

734. What were the most victories the Huskers have had in one season, including bowl victories?

735. When was the first time that Nebraska played a football game outside of the United States?

736. After the 1970 team won the national championship, who came to Lincoln to pay tribute to Bob Devaney and his team?

737. Nebraska in 1994 had the misfortune of meeting two consecutive teams in the final home game for their respective coaches. Who were these teams?

738. Where did Nebraska play its home games prior to the 1923 season when Memorial Stadium was completed?

739. In which season did Nebraska play its 1000th football game?

740. When was the Big Six Conference formed and who were the member teams?

741. What was the fewest number of home games won by Nebraska in a season?

742. In 1939 the Huskers defeated two formidable teams, the first time they had beaten them both in the same season. Who were these two teams that always gave the Huskers fits in the early days?

734. Nebraska won 13 games in 1971 when it won the national championship with a 13-0-0 record and again in 1994 when they finished 13-0-0 and were crowned national champions.

735. The Coca-Cola Bowl played against Kansas State on December 5, 1992 was held in Tokyo, Japan. The Huskers defeated the Wildcats, 38-24, to claim the Big Eight championship.

736. None other than President Richard Nixon flew to Lincoln and joined in the celebration and publicly congratulated Devaney for his team's accomplishments.

737. The Huskers struggled against Iowa State, 28-12, in Jim Walden's swan song and then went to Norman and defeated Gary Gibbs' Sooners, 13-3. Talk about tough Husker luck!!

738. Old Nebraska Field, which ran east and west just south of Memorial Stadium, was Nebraska's old home field.

739. On November 6, 1993, the Huskers defeated Kansas in its 1000th contest. It is fitting that the milestone was reached against Kansas since the rivalry with the Jayhawks is Nebraska's longest at 101 games as of 1994.

740. In 1928, when Kansas, Kansas State, Missouri, Oklahoma, Iowa State and Nebraska pulled out of the Missouri Valley Conference to form a new group, the Big Six was born. Nebraska won the first conference title in football.

741. During the bad old days the Huskers were winless at home in 1947, 1951 and 1957.

742. In 1939 the Huskers defeated powerhouses Minnesota 6-0 and Pittsburgh 14-13. One or the other had always spoiled the previous Husker seasons.

743. In a four year span from 1990 to 1994 how many teams did Nebraska face that finished the season #1 in the polls?

744. Nebraska played in the first college game where two teams entered the contest ranked the same in the Associated Press poll. When did this happen and who was the opponent?

745. What is the longest losing streak in Nebraska's football history?

746. What was N.U.'s only blemish on its record in the 1970 national championship season?

747. When did the Nebraska Cornhusker marching band begin playing at football games?

748. In 1962 when the team won its first two games, how long had it been since that had happened?

749. What was the greatest number of home games lost by Nebraska in a single season?

750. Who was the first Nebraska player to leave school early to enter the NFL draft?

751. Prior to 1962, Devaney's first season, how many consecutive seasons had the Huskers suffered through at least one shutout during each season?

743. The Huskers had the misfortune of going up against five teams that owned a piece of the national championship. As you might have guessed, they lost all five games. The teams involved were Colorado, Georgia Tech, Washington, Miami of Florida and Florida State.

744. When Nebraska faced Colorado on October 31, 1992 both teams were tied for 8th in the AP poll. Nebraska demolished the Buffaloes 52-7 in Lincoln.

745. The longest losing skein was 7 games in the 1957 season.

746. A 21-21 tie with Southern California in the second game of the season was the only blemish. This tie was followed by 10 straight wins in 1970 and, of course, the national title.

747. This tradition goes back as far as the very beginnings of the sport at Nebraska, 1890.

748. Nebraska had not won its first two games since 1952, 10 years before the arrival of Bob Devaney in Lincoln.

749. Lest we forget the less successful Nebraska seasons, ponder this: the Huskers lost all five home games in 1947, 1951 and 1957.

750. Johnny Mitchell, the great Husker tight end, decided to leave after his sophomore year and was drafted in the first round of the 1992 pro draft by the New York Jets.

751. The Huskers had 7 consecutive seasons of such indignities. In 1955 they were shut out 3 times, one time in 1956, 4 times in 1957, 3 times in 1958, 2 times in 1959, 2 times in 1960 and 2 times in 1961. Nebraska had been shut out 17 times in 70 games, 1955-61.

752. Before Devaney's era, what was the last Nebraska team to win 9 games in a season?

753. Who was the second Husker player to leave school early to enter the pro draft?

754. How long was Nebraska's unbeaten streak from 1969 to 1972?

755. How many years did Lyell Bremser broadcast the Nebraska football games on KFAB radio?

756. During which season did N.U. establish the record for largest home game attendance?

757. During the 1990 season Nebraska had the dubious distinction of losing to both teams that shared the national championship. Name those two teams.

758. What year did Nebraska last have a winning season before the arrival of Bob Devaney?

759. What was the last game that Nebraska was involved in which was forfeited by one of the teams?

760. In 1991 Nebraska again had the dubious distinction of losing to both teams that shared the national championship. Name those teams.

752. The last time that a Husker team had won as many as 9 games in a season was in 1905 when the team went 9-2-0

753. Derek Brown, half of the "We Backs" followed Johnny Mitchell's lead the year before and entered the pro draft in 1993 after his junior year. He was selected in the fourth round by the New Orleans Saints.

754. The Huskers had an impressive string of 33 games without a loss from the loss to Missouri in 1969 to the loss to UCLA at the beginning of the 1972 season.

755. "Mr. Football" did the play-by-play for KFAB for 45 years, 1939-83. During that time Bremser never missed a single Husker game, a truly remarkable achievement.

756. In 1988 an average of 76,342 fans attended six Nebraska home games to establish the season record.

757. The Huskers had earlier lost to AP champion, Colorado, 27-12, in November. In the Florida Citrus Bowl, the Georgia Tech Yellow Jackets crushed the Huskers 45-21 and claimed the UPI national title.

758. The last taste of success that Nebraska had before the Devaney years came in 1954 when the Huskers went 6-5-0, including the crushing defeat by Duke in the Orange Bowl.

759. The last time the Huskers were involved in a forfeited game was in 1951 when N.U. was awarded a game against Kansas State, 1-0, by forfeit. On the playing field the score ended up tied 6-6.

760. Nebraska had lost to USA Today/CNN champion Washington 36-21 in September and then were crushed by AP champ Miami 22-0 in the 1992 Federal Express Orange Bowl.

761. How many unbeaten home seasons has Nebraska had in the history of Memorial Stadium?

762. When was artificial turf first installed in Memorial Stadium?

763. When Nebraska tied for the Big Eight Championship in 1969, why didn't the team go to the Orange Bowl and which team did represent the Big Eight?

764. Not surprisingly, one team owns four spots on the all-time top 10 opponents scoring games against Nebraska. Who is this team?

765. How many perfect home seasons has Nebraska had in Memorial Stadium?

766. The Huskers suffered two of their three losses in 1974 when a pivotal player was injured and unable to continue. Who was this key individual?

767. Who was the first black athlete at Nebraska?

768. State Senator Ernie Chambers of Omaha has tried unsuccessfully to get a bill passed in the state legislature which would directly affect N.U. football players. What does his bill propose?

769. Why was N.U. declared the Big Eight champion of 1972?

761. Through 1994 the Huskers have recorded 25 unbeaten home seasons in Memorial Stadium, which was completed in 1923.

762. The Astroturf was first installed in 1970.

763. The Huskers couldn't go to Miami because they were tied for the conference crown with Missouri, who had defeated N.U. 17-7 earlier in the season. The Huskers went to the Sun Bowl instead and crushed Georgia 45-6.

764. Nebraska's old nemesis, Oklahoma scored 55 points against the Huskers in 1954, 54 in 1956, 49 in 1950 and 48 points in 1949.

765. Through 1994 the Huskers have recorded 20 perfect home seasons in Memorial Stadium which was completed in 1923.

766. Dave Humm suffered a hip pointer against Wisconsin in a 21-20 setback and he was knocked unconscious in the 21-10 loss to Missouri, a game in which the Tigers scored three times in the fourth quarter.

767. George Flippin, 1891-1894, was also only the fifth black athlete at a white university in the nation.

768. Chambers wants to have the state declare N.U. football players as state employees and to pay them for their service on the field. The bill has failed several times.

769. The Huskers were champions because Oklahoma was put on probation for recruiting violations and was forced to forfeit three league victories.

770. After one particularly memorable win, all of the members of an N.U. football team were made admirals in the Nebraska Navy. Which game produced such high praise?

771. During which game did the Huskers, for the only time in team history, wear blue uniforms?

772. In the period between the Rose Bowl team and the arrival of Bob Devaney in 1962, how many winning seasons did the Huskers have?

773. In the first 51 years of football at Nebraska, 1890-1940, how many losing seasons did they have?

774. Who is considered by most observers to be Nebraska's most famous walkon player?

775. When was Nebraska's first night home game?

776. In what year did Nebraska win its first conference championship under Bob Devaney's leadership?

777. What was Nebraska's most successful decade in football?

770. Such honors could only have resulted from the astounding 1959 upset victory over Oklahoma, 25-21, which snapped the Sooners' long conference string in which they were unbeaten in 75 games.

771. Nebraska donned the blue uniforms for the 1923 game against Oklahoma. The change must have been a good one as the Huskers blanked the Sooners 24-0.

772. The Huskers experienced only three winning seasons during those 21 years. They went 6-2-1 in 1950, 5-4-1 in 1952 and 6-5-0 in 1954. Those were the only semi-bright spots during a wasteland of football hardships for Nebraska.

773. Nebraska only experienced two losing seasons in the first 51 years. The team went 2-7-1 in the 1899 campaign and 2-3-1 in 1918.

774. Running back I.M. Hipp, who went on to star at Nebraska and lettered 1977-79, made a lot of headlines as a Husker walkon and probably influenced a number of other players to walk on at Nebraska.

775. The Huskers met Florida State under the lights at Home in 1986. They won the game 34-17. Ironically, this was Nebraska's last victory over the Seminoles.

776. N.U. won the championship in 1963 and ended the season with a 10-1-0 record.

777. The Huskers had a golden decade 1980-89 during which they had a record of 103-20-0 for a winning percentage of .837 and represents an average of over 10 wins a year.

778. How many games in a row did Nebraska win from 1970 to 1972?

779. Who were the co-captains of the great 1971 national championship team?

780. What was the worst win-loss record for a season by a Nebraska football team in the history of the sport at the school and when was this dubious record established?

781. What game marked the 200th consecutive sellout at Memorial Stadium?

782. How many times has Nebraska played 12 games in the regular season?

783. When was Nebraska's first national television appearance?

784. When Nebraska crushed Colorado 69-19 in 1983 it established an NCAA scoring record. What was it?

785. When Nebraska won the national championship in 1971, who finished 2nd and 3rd in the polls?

786. In the great 1994 regular season Nebraska trailed only once at halftime--to an unlikely opponent. Which team accomplished this feat?

778. The awesome Husker machine had won 23 straight games from the tie with Southern California in 1970 to the loss to UCLA at the start of the 1972 season.

779. The two do-captains were Jerry Tagge, quarterback, and Jim Anderson, defensive back.

780. The Huskers reached their low point in 1957 when they had a record of 1-9-0 with only a 14-7 victory over Kansas State as a bright spot.

781. In perhaps Nebraska's most complete game of the year, the Huskers dominated Colorado 24-7 on October 29, 1994 to mark the 200th consecutive sellout.

782. The Huskers have played 12 games in the regular season six times; in 1971, 1976, 1982, 1983, 1988 and 1994.

783. The Huskers were first televised in the September 19, 1953 home game in Lincoln against Oregon. Nebraska lost the contest 20-12.

784. They scored the most points in a short period of possession time, namely, 41 points in a span of 2 minutes and 55 seconds. Imagine—six touchdowns and 5 extra points in less than three minutes of possession time.

785. Oklahoma finished 2nd and Colorado finished 3rd, the only time in history that three teams from one conference finished the season 1-2-3. Alabama, another Husker victim, finished 4th in the polls.

786. Wyoming, a big underdog, surprised the Huskers by jumping out to a 14-0 lead and held a 21-14 advantage at the intermission. Fortunately, Nebraska was able to regroup and pull out a 42-32 victory.

787. At which non-bowl game did Nebraska play before the largest crowd?

788. In what year did Memorial Stadium open?

789. How many times had Nebraska been ranked in AP's final ratings before Devaney's arrival in 1962?

790. Name the Husker basketball center who in 1987 decided to give football a try and the position he played.

791. Early in 1994 the Big Eight Conference reached an agreement with four Southwest Conference teams to join the Conference in 1996. Name these four teams.

792. What was the first father and son combination to both letter in football at Nebraska?

793. What did Don Bryant do before coming to work as sports information director at Nebraska?

794. In what year did Nebraska first win a Big Eight conference football championship?

795. When did the Huskers surprise their fans by donning all-red uniforms for a game?

796. What was similar about the great 1983 Nebraska team and the 1994 Penn State team?

787. The attendance record was set when the Huskers played at University Park, Pa, on September 25, 1982 in a contest with Penn State, 85,304 saw the Huskers lose that game 27-24 to the Nittany Lions.

788. Memorial Stadium was completed in 1923 and first used in the 1923 season.

789. The Huskers finished in the rankings twice. They were 9th in 1936 and 7th in 1940.

790. Keith Neubert not only was a good enough athlete to play at tight end he earned a football letter in 1987.

791. Texas, Texas Tech, Texas A&M and Baylor will add tremendous influence and excitement to the new league, the Big 12 Conference.

792. Grove Porter lettered in 1914 as a halfback. His son, Morton, earned a letter as a guard in 1943.

793. Bryant was sports editor of the Lincoln Star before coming to N.U. in 1963. Since coming to Nebraska, he has done everything he could to promote all Husker sports, men's and women's.

794. Nebraska won its first Big Eight championship in 1963, Bob Devaney's second season at N.U.

795. Nebraska tried this ploy in the annual shootout with Oklahoma in 1986. Unfortunately, the outcome was not so sweet, a 20-17 loss to the Sooners in Lincoln.

796. Like the 1983 Husker team, the 1994 Penn State team had a superb offense, tops in the nation, and an average defense. Ironically, both teams finished the season #2 in the polls.

797. Three ex-Huskers played for the champion of Super Bowl XXIV after the 1989 season. Name the players and the team.

798. A Nebraska All-American almost won a medal in the infamous 1936 Berlin Olympics. Who was this player and in which event did he compete?

799. When were the Huskers last shut out in Memorial Stadium?

800. Who is the third Nebraska Cornhusker to leave school early to enter the NFL draft?

797. Roger Craig, Tom Rathman and Jamie Williams were all a part of the San Francisco 49ers' winning effort in Super Bowl XXIV.

798. Husker fullback Sam Francis came oh-so-close in finishing 4th in the shot put in Berlin.

799. An unlikely team accomplished this feat. Kansas State shut out Nebraska 12-0 in 1968 during the second of Bob Devaney's dismal 6-4-0 seasons. No other team has held the Huskers scoreless at home in 25 years.

800. Calvin Jones, after the 1993 season, decided to follow the leads of Johnny Mitchell and Derek Brown and declared himself eligible for the 1994 pro draft. He was drafted in the third round by the Los Angeles Raiders.

Johnny Mitchell